DEVELOPING EMOTIONALLY LITERATE STAFF

DEVELOPING EMOTIONALLY LITERATE STAFF

A Practical Guide

Elizabeth Morris and Julie Casey

Paul Chapman
Publishing

Paul Chapman Publishing
A SAGE Publications Company
1 Oliver's Yard
55 City Road
London EC1Y 1SP

SAGE Publications Inc
2455 Teller Road
Thousand Oaks, California 91320

SAGE Publications India Pvt Ltd
B-42, Panchsheel Enclave
Post Box 4109
New Delhi 110 017

Library of Congress Control Number: 2005934978

A catalogue record for this book is available from the British Library

ISBN 1-4129-1039-0
ISBN 1-4129-1040-4 (pbk)

Typeset by Pantek Arts Ltd, Maidstone, Kent
Printed in Great Britain by Cromwell Press, Trowbridge, Wilts
Printed on paper from sustainable resources

CONTENTS

ACKNOWLEDGEMENTS

The sections I have written for this book are dedicated to the memory of Chris Lindup, respected colleague, friend and endless source of inspiration. Special thanks to Dr Robin Banerjee and the staff at Winston's Wish, Gloucestershire, for allowing me to draw so freely on their enormous expertise, to friends and colleagues Sally Whittingham, Maggie Walker, Brigid Allen and Jean Gross for their intellect, integrity and generosity of spirit. Thanks also to my wonderful family for their patience and the endless supply of ready-meals and love, and lastly to Simon for sustaining me with his humour and wit during the long nights of redrafting.

Julie Casey

My parts in this book would not have been possible without the unstinting generosity and patience of a great number of people – family, friends and colleagues included. For material and examples of what works, and what does not, I particularly thank all my students on the Certificate programme in Emotional Literacy. They all have a passion for the topic and share their professional successes and 'learning opportunities' with me and each other in a perfect example of collaboration and support. For practical help in keeping my feet on the ground and getting the right things in the right places at the right time, my personal assistant Rachel Carter has been a source of irreplaceable support. For his editing and critical analytical skills (which include taking his life in his hands when questioning some of my more deeply felt, but often untested, ideas), Tim Sparrow has been both brave and invaluable! Finally my thanks and love, as always, go to my niece, Rachael Morris, and nephew, Robbie Morris, who have provided unstinting emotional support with their encouragement and love, even though they have no idea what I'm writing about!

Elizabeth Morris

The authors and publisher are grateful for permission to use the following:

Activity 7.5 from Corrie, C. (2003) *Becoming Emotionally Intelligent*, Network Educational Press, London (www.networkpress.co.uk)

Resource Sheet 1: Maslow's hierarchy of needs from *Toward a Psychology of Being* (1999) Maslow, A.H., et al. Reproduced with permission of John Wiley & Sons, Inc

Resource Sheet 2: Relevance, Readiness and Resource from Fullan, M. (1991) *The New Meaning of Educational Change*, Cassell, London

Chris Walker for the illustrations on pages 51, 59, 62, 73, 81, 102 and 113

ABOUT THE AUTHORS

Dr Elizabeth Morris, Principal of the School of Emotional Literacy, is a psychologist and specialist in the provision of emotional education. She is a member of the DfES advisory practitioner group on social and emotional competence development and was a developmental psychology consultant during the writing of the SEAL resource for the National Primary Strategy. She is the emotional literacy consultant for the National Positive Mental Health and Well-being programme in Scotland and advisor on emotionally literate approaches for Edinburgh's Children and Families Service. Elizabeth created the first post-graduate level certificate and advanced diploma in emotional literacy with Bristol University and her programme now runs throughout the UK. She trains and consults on emotional literacy internationally, visiting American, South African and European conferences in emotional education and mental health regularly to give keynote addresses and workshops on systemic and operational applications of emotional literacy development in schools and families. She has written extensively on self esteem and emotional literacy development and has books published in both Australia and the UK.

In this book **Julie Casey** draws upon her wealth of practical and theoretical knowledge and experience in bringing together the three fields of education, emotional literacy and continuing professional development (CPD) for teachers and educational practitioners. In 1995 she achieved the award of 'Britain's Best Teacher' having spent sixteen years in the field of primary education. During this time she also obtained a first class degree in psychology, followed by an M.Ed in Educational Psychology, subsequently working in this field with individuals, groups and organizations as a specialist in Behaviour and Emotional Literacy. She is currently undertaking a doctorate at Bristol University looking at effective practice in teacher's CPD in the area of social and emotional learning. She is a published author in the field and has written for the Council of Europe on reducing violence in schools. Recently Julie has played a major role in the development and co-ordination of the Primary Strategy curriculum materials for developing children's social, emotional and behavioural skills ('Excellence and Enjoyment: social and emotional aspects of learning'), as well as leading the development of the National Behaviour and Attendance Audit for KS1 and KS2, and contributing to a range of training materials for the DfES including the Primary Strategy and the National Programme of School Leadership – Behaviour and Attendance. For the past two years she has been a key member of the Government's practitioner body which supports and advises the DfES on issues related to Emotional Literacy and social, emotional and behavioural skills in schools. In addition, Julie lectures in emotional literacy development at Bristol University on the post-graduate level certificate in Emotional Literacy, and works as a consultant to clients such as the BBC, local education authorities and a range of educational organizations. Julie has four children and lives in Somerset.

GLOSSARY

CBT	cognitive behavioural therapy
CPD	continuing professional development
DfES	Department for Education and Skills
EHWB	emotional health and well-being
EL	emotional literacy
KS1/2/3	Key stage 1/2/3
LEA	local education authority
LSA	learning support assistant
NHSS	National Healthy Schools Standard
PNS	Primary National Strategy
PRU	Pupil Referral Unit
PSHE	personal, social and health education
SEAL	social and emotional aspects of learning
SEBS	social, emotional and behavioural skills
SEL	social and emotional learning
SLT	senior leadership team

INTRODUCTION

A note on terminology

The plethora of terms used to describe the skills involved in 'emotional literacy' reflects the multi-disciplinary origins of the concept. Often the terminology used gives a clue to its origin – the field of psychology, for example, has given us 'emotional intelligence' while those coming from a health-related perspective are likely to refer to 'emotional health and well-being' (EHWB), with educationalists often preferring 'emotional literacy' or referring to 'personal, social and health education'.

In this publication we have chosen primarily to use the term 'social and emotional learning' (SEL), but also follow the conventions of the Department for Education and Skills (DfES) in talking about 'social and emotional aspects of learning' (SEAL) and 'social, emotional and behavioural skills' (SEBS) where these are more appropriate to the context. We take 'emotionally literate' behaviour to be behaviour in which positive SEBS are displayed.

The concepts of emotional literacy are applicable to all contexts where children and young people are educated. We use the term 'school' or 'organization' in the widest possible sense to include PRUs, nursery settings, specialist residential settings and so on. For this reason we also refer generally to 'staff' or 'adults' rather than 'teachers', and include all adults working with children and young people within an organization.

Finally we have chosen to refer to 'children and young people' in order to promote a holistic view of the individual existing within a variety of contexts, although we also use 'pupil' when referring specifically to a school setting.

About this book

Aims and objectives

The aim of this development manual is to equip all staff with the competence, confidence and motivation to facilitate social and emotional learning in children and young people, both through an explicit 'taught' programme and through the creation and maintenance of a supportive ethos and environment congruent with the learning that the programme promotes. Specific learning objectives are detailed for each training module in Chapter 4.

The book consists of:

- an overview of the area of social and emotional learning (Introduction)

- a rationale for the importance of staff development in this area (Introduction)

- an overview of critical success factors and principles for implementing a staff development programme (Chapter 1)

- a model 'framework for implementation' that takes into account all of these success factors and enables successful strategic planning via a step-by-step process. The framework includes a suggested time frame, task analysis and sample resource sheets to support each step, with all of these based on the experiences of many schools (Chapter 2)

- information to enable the coordinator or training facilitator to put together an appropriate professional development programme to meet the needs of their own individual context, guidance on structuring safe and effective staff group sessions and a range of samples 'starting and ending activities' for motivating and engaging an overloaded staff, as well as ideas for supporting staff learning between sessions (for example, through setting up a coaching programme) (Chapter 3)

- ten training 'modules' with suggested activities for use with staff groups to develop what staff need to know, understand and be able to do, in order to work effectively with children and young people in the area of social and emotional learning (Chapter 4). Each session focuses on an area of SEL (for example, conflict management; relationship skills; working as a team) and provides:

- background knowledge plus useful concepts and models (some as pre-session tasks or readings which give participants an opportunity to consider how the subject matter 'fits' with what they know already, and to formulate questions, ideas, examples and so on)

- a chance to explore and respond to the content at an adult level

- an opportunity to build up an individual, confidential profile of strengths and weaknesses in emotional literacy (with support in further interpreting these)

- the option of applying this learning to classroom and whole-school practice

- opportunities for feedback and reflection, and to consolidate and embed learning through 'intersessional' tasks

- links to the DfES SEAL cross-curricular materials (Primary Strategy, 2005) and other useful resources

- a focus on 'whole-school aspects' to develop.

Process

School leadership teams will find it useful to read through the Introduction, critical success factors and underlying principles (Chapter 1), and to consider individually the implications of the steps outlined in the 'Framework for Intervention' (Chapter 2), before coming together to consider the feasibility of an initial commitment to the initiative (sometimes using the resource sheets provided to make that decision). Once the initial commitment has been made, the 'framework' will prove useful for the strategic planning of each step of the process, which is generally delegated to an appointed 'coordinator' or training facilitator who reports back to the SLT (Senior Leadership Team) at agreed junctures.

The book is designed to be:

- easy to use

- comprehensive – with all information sheets, worksheets, checklists and case-studies provided as resource sheets or within the appendix

- based on an effective model of professional development.

The model of professional development

The programme is collaborative, with a whole-school focus sustained over time. A recent review of research on effective, collaborative CPD (Continuing Professional Development) for teachers of the 5–16 age range (Cordingley et al., 2003) concluded that this model of CPD had positive effects on:

- teachers' attitudes and beliefs (including those about their self-efficacy – their ability to affect pupils' learning and increased confidence in their own learning)

- teaching strategies and practices (staff were more willing to try out new ideas in their practice and demonstrated a greater commitment to changing practice)

- students' attitudes and behaviours

- students' achievements.

The study also identified common features of successful CPD interventions and each of these has been included as an option within the programme. Examples of successful features of CPD include:

- observation with professional dialogue including feedback (e.g. a coaching model)

- processes to encourage, extend and structure professional dialogue (pre-reading and sessions within each module specifically provide these opportunities)

- processes for sustaining CPD over time to enable teachers to embed learning in their own classroom settings (intersessional tasks, a reflective learning log and the coaching process all promote the embedding of learning) (Cordingley et al., 2003).

What is social and emotional learning and what has it got to do with schools?

Social and emotional learning is generally considered to inhabit two broad domains: emotional or 'intrapersonal' learning covers the areas of learning that enable us to know and understand ourselves – to recognize and identify our feelings, to know our strengths and weaknesses, our preferences, beliefs and values, what motivates us and how we learn best, and to apply this self-knowledge to our choices and actions. It is this intrapersonal learning that underpins our ability to manage our feelings and to become internally motivated, self-directed individuals, able to take responsibility for our own behaviour and learning and to demonstrate persistence and resilience in the face of setbacks, failure or disappointment.

Learning within the social domain (or 'interpersonal' learning) enables us to form social relationships, to cooperate with others, to resolve disagreements, solve problems and to celebrate and respect the similarities and differences between us. The fundamental skill for social learning is empathy – the ability to understand others.

Thus there is a strong case to be made for the intrinsic value of social and emotional learning within education. Children and young people would (and many do) struggle to negotiate their way through the social and emotional demands of the school day without them. They represent those 'skills for life' which are necessary not just within schools, but in home, work and community contexts.

But there is also the value of social and emotional learning that we might term 'instrumental'. Daniel Goleman (1995) provides a robust body of evidence that links emotional intelligence to success in all domains of life. Of great relevance to schools, there is now a growing amount of evidence that academic learning itself (often viewed as the 'legitimate' remit of schools) is improved when social and emotional factors are explicitly addressed (Petrides et al., 2004).

This evidence lifts social and emotional learning firmly out of the 'deficit' model of this work (as a specialist provision for children with special needs in this area) and into the mainstream arena. The promotion of the 'Social and emotional aspects of learning (SEAL)' cross-curriculum materials in the UK (DfES, 2005) as an entitlement curriculum for *all* children attests to this change in status, as do references to the domains of emotional literacy in the Primary National Strategy (PNS) professional development materials *Conditions for Learning* (DfES, 2004a) and *Progression in Key Aspects of Learning* (DfES, 2004a).

> *Today's educators have a renewed perspective on what common sense always suggested: when schools attend systematically to students' social and emotional skills, the academic achievement of children increases, the incidence of problem behaviours decreases, and the quality of the relationships surrounding each child improves. And, students become the productive, responsible, contributing members of society that we all want…Thus, social and emotional education is sometimes called the missing piece, that part of the mission of the school that, while always close to the thoughts of many teachers, somehow eluded them.* (Elias et al., 1997)

Putting in place a taught curriculum focusing on social and emotional learning, within a school ethos that values and consolidates this work, therefore pays important dividends. There is nothing else in the current educational world that is linked to so many significant educational agendas.

Improving learning and achievement

The key role of emotional factors in the process of learning itself (and its consequent impact on the standards agenda) has only recently been recognized. In brief, the 'emotional brain' plays a central role in accessing; 'fixing' and recalling information as every piece of sensory information that enters a pupil's mind is immediately tagged with an emotional label. That happens before it enters the higher circuits of cognitive thought and memory. Students will remember and easily make sense of information that comes tagged with pleasurable emotions, rather than that which is linked with the uncomfortable.

Improving behaviour

Behaviour is another educational agenda that is connected with emotional literacy. Every behaviour pattern is driven by an emotional state. Often the behaviours that are experienced as more challenging happen when a student has no effective strategy for handling an underlying emotion. Perhaps this is because they have not learnt or rehearsed a variety of strategies, supported by a developing understanding and awareness of their emotional states. This means that they are left with little option but to act out, sublimate or deny how they feel.

Attendance

Attendance at school has many emotional associations. Pupils who opt to stay away or remove themselves from school are usually driven by strong emotions. For them school may be an environment where they feel hopeless and helpless, where they have no sense of belonging and believe that they have little to offer. Alternatively, they may be positively drawn to environments other than school where they do feel valued (with peers), or to subcultures where they can use the strengths they believe they have, such as reading the social dynamics amongst adults on the street and using that knowledge to profit financially and gain 'street cred'. This then leads into the crime agenda that is another key issue both socially and politically.

Inclusion

A strong agenda over recent years has been that of inclusion which also has distinct links with emotional and social aspects of learning. The emotional state of a class is affected by the emotional state of each individual within it. Students who struggle to access learning for a wide variety of reasons or are victims of stereotyping and victimization can end up in emotional states that are very destructive to themselves – and perhaps to others. Modelling the celebration of diversity, openness and acceptance and building the skill of empathy can do much to soothe the intensity of emotions in classrooms and facilitate inclusion.

Teacher recruitment and retention

Finally, teacher recruitment and retention is an educational agenda strongly linked to social and emotional factors. Where behaviour and attendance are poor, staff feel disempowered and demotivated. Both staff and students end up feeling insecure and threatened, in an environment which must be secure for learning and teaching to take place. Frequently staff leave in a state of emotional ill-health; stressed and unhappy, angry and bitter. At the same time, the social status of teachers has dropped and this adds to the emotional pressure on remaining staff.

In order to counteract these effects, the focus on emotional literacy needs to extend to the emotional health and well-being of the staff themselves. With support and opportunities to develop their own emotional literacy, the emotional climate of a school can become one of safety and respect. Schools which focus on the emotional health and well-being of staff (as well as that of pupils) are less likely to experience recruitment and retention difficulties and are more likely to have better attendance records amongst staff. They are therefore also less likely to need to find cover for staff amongst a rapidly diminishing pool of labour, with all the attendant 'fall-out', disruption and pressure.

Aren't we already doing it?

Social and emotional learning is not something that we are presenting as new to schools. There is much excellent practice that already promotes it and many professionals have been fundamentally involved in developing and improving this area of education for many years. Much of the subject matter of social and emotional learning is the explicit (though not exclusive) focus of, for example, the Foundation Stage personal, social and emotional area of learning, Religious Education, assemblies, and the transpose acronym and definition: Pers., Soc., and Health Ed. (PSHE)/citizenship Personal, Social and Health Education (PSHE)/citizenship curriculum. Many schools develop the area further through the NHSS (National Healthy Schools Standard) and by using circle time, philosophy for children (P4C), the provision of school counsellors, peer mediation schemes and so on. It is important that whatever work is undertaken in schools builds upon existing staff skills and complements what is in place already.

The existence of this expertise and good practice begs the question: Do we really need a stronger focus on these aspects of learning? The authors' work with schools which have implemented a range of environmental and taught programmes designed to improve pupils' social and emotional skills (including the PNS SEAL materials (DfES, 2005) suggests that this is indeed the case. Some examples of 'additionality' as identified by schools (many listed by those who were already judged to be performing well in this area) include:

- a heightened profile and status for social and emotional learning

- the 'legitimizing' of this area of work when talking to governors, parents and other stakeholders

- the use of the programme as an overarching framework to encompass and give coherence to other initiatives already in place with greater consistency throughout the school (in both formal and informal contexts) in the language used to speak to children and the way that behavioural incidents are handled

- a sense of individual and corporate responsibility at all levels of school life towards focusing on the social and emotional aspects of learning (as opposed to the previous assumption that such matters were the sole responsibility of the PSHE coordinator) and with greater clarity about specific aims leading to more consistency of practice

- greater credibility arising from working to a clear and rigorous set of learning intentions (in an area in which aims and objectives have been somewhat 'slippery')

- Increased progress in children's knowledge, understanding and skills in the area of social and emotional learning when a spiral curriculum enables staff to build upon children's existing skills, as opposed to the sporadic progress noted when more 'ad hoc' arrangements were in place.

Why focus on the adults?

The aim of a taught social and emotional development programme is to focus children and adults on the social and emotional aspects of learning (SEAL) and help children and young people to develop social, emotional and behavioural skills, knowledge and understanding (SEBS). Children and young people need these to manage both socially and academically, at school and beyond. As educators we are doing more than imparting a body of discrete knowledge; we are attempting to develop compassionate, responsible, creative and cooperative citizens for tomorrow's world. So why is it so necessary to train staff for this task when we have seen that much of it is already taking place?

Providing staff with development opportunities and training in the area of social and emotional learning is critical to successful learning in this area for children and young people for the three main reasons outlined below.

1 Staff development opportunities help to bring about a supportive, warm and encouraging environment.

This is related to the important role of school environment. Because the primary content area of social and emotional learning is the child or young person, and the desired outcome is an ability to *use* social, emotional and behavioural knowledge, understanding and skills in ways that maximize life opportunities, there are implications for structuring the overall environment to support the learning that does not arise in relation to other, more traditional subject areas.

Within the social and emotional curriculum we might, for example, explore strategies for conflict resolution, building friendships and managing difficult feelings, but the real learning happens with the repeated application of these within the wider environment which establishes new responses in place of the 'default' settings from earlier learning. In order to support the development and consolidation of the skills we focus on within the social and emotional curriculum, we need to provide a 'learners' environment' – somewhere that feels safe for children to take a risk, to put into practice and 'try out' their developing skills and understanding. We might liken this to the adult experience of learning to drive a car – we recognize the need to learn, practise and consolidate skills in the safety of little used back-streets; we don't send learners out on the motorway to practise! And how much greater is the need for safety when the object of our focus is not something we do, but how we are as individuals with all the vulnerabilities which we fear may be exposed?

The importance of the environment is not restricted to 'learners', however. Even as professional skilled adults our ability to deploy our social and emotional skills varies on a continuum from sophistication to incompetence depending on context. In a new environment, in situations in which we feel threatened or disliked, in times of stress, exhaustion and uncertainty, even the most emotionally literate adult can find themselves behaving in emotionally 'illiterate' ways.

One compelling reason for developing staff knowledge, skills and understanding in the area of emotional literacy is therefore to enable them to structure a facilitative environment – a task which requires an understanding of the environmental factors that facilitate or hinder the development of children's and young people's social and emotional learning.

2 Staff development opportunities support adults' ability to 'model' emotionally literate ways of behaving.

Of the many factors that contribute to the overall ethos or environment of the school, that which has the greatest significance in encouraging pupils to apply their learning and consolidate their skills is the adult modelling that they experience (the way we interact with pupils and with each other, the language we use, the way we demonstrate that we value ourselves and others). You may have come across these wise words:

> *Don't worry that you do not think the children are listening to you; worry that they are watching everything you do.*

Typically, adults working in education have had little input in this crucial area and few explicit opportunities to explore or develop their own skills, knowledge and understanding – essential prerequisites for modelling emotionally literate behaviour.

Staff who hold attitudes of empathy, respect, openness and optimism create a fertile environment for pupils to easily absorb much of the social and emotional learning they will require. An essential element of that positive attitude is confidence. For staff to teach or model good SEBS, they need to feel confident about why they are doing what they are doing and their level of competence.

Although the focus is on developing the professional skills which will enable them to support children, pilot studies suggest that the skills, knowledge and understanding covered in the training materials are often experienced as engaging, motivating and fun because of their relevance to life outside of school.

3 To develop staff ownership, confidence and competence in delivering the taught social and emotional curriculum.

As with any 'subject matter', staff will benefit from the opportunity provided by staff meetings or inset sessions to familiarize themselves with the materials and suggested teaching styles and structures. Research suggests (Goleman, 1998) that the most effective learning opportunities for developing SEBS involve participative, experiential and interactive activities which prompt individuals to engage at a personal level and to construct their own understanding. Some staff may already feel comfortable with these teaching styles and use them across the curriculum, while for others they may present new and potentially threatening challenges.

Evidence from the authors' experiences and from the schools involved in the PNS SEAL pilot suggests that having opportunities for focusing explicitly on, and 'trying out' such experiential methods, has a significant impact on staff attitudes and willingness to adopt such strategies in the classroom. The suggested training plan provides such opportunities for staff.

A further and more fundamental reason for offering staff development opportunities in this area lies again in the differences between the nature of the content matter for social and emotional programmes and more 'academic' subject matter. The content areas covered in social and emotional programmes often elicit strong emotional responses in adults as well as children and young people – there are very few of us, for example, who have not been touched in some way by loss or bullying. For this reason, we need to ensure that adults have had the opportunity to engage with, explore and experience the material at an adult level in order to become aware of, and be able to deal with, their own responses before working with children.

This is not something that can be learnt from a book and repackaged in child-sized bites. Because our emotions and social relationships are so integral to being human we need to feel the lessons with 'all of us' so that they become part of who we are. The experience of going through some of the material with a more personal focus helps us become aware of our own strengths and those areas for development in emotional literacy.

Experiences enable us to become aware of and consider our beliefs which in turn shape our responses. For example, if we believe that children are actually very skilled in these matters and are choosing to not use their skills productively we will feel angry and frustrated and have a negative attitude. We may even underplay lessons in these areas because we believe that they will make little difference. However, if we believe that children are doing their best with the resources they have and that for whatever reason they do not possess the full resources needed in these fields, we will be more likely to have a positive attitude and feel interested and determined. The process of becoming 'emotionally literate' as an individual or as an organization must engage both hearts and minds.

PART 1 IMPLEMENTING A SUCCESSFUL SEL INITIATIVE

CHAPTER 1

Establishing the Conditions for Success

The aim of this book is to equip staff to be ready, willing and able to deliver a taught SEBS/SEAL curriculum effectively. As with any initiative, it will have champions and detractors. It will also have to compete with all the other issues and agendas fighting for time and attention. So in order to prepare the ground to ensure that the initiative becomes embedded, it is helpful to consider all the aspects that have been shown to underlie a successful implementation. It will also help to consider any sabotage or pitfall that might occur and prepare in advance for this.

Critical success factors

Commitment at senior leadership level

This is a 'must have'. Commitment at this level means that support will be available to make the inevitable tweaks and changes, adaptations and additions that will need to happen. Commitment from senior managers means that the integration of the principles of emotional literacy will have priority in a school. Thus in the jostle for attention and energy the emotional literacy agenda will continue to be an important consideration. Where senior managers have the underlying belief that this approach will improve standards, behaviour, attendance and the emotional well-being of the school community, it is more likely to become a reality.

But commitment means more than support; it also means leadership. Senior members of staff, for example, will lead by modelling their own commitment to personal emotional health and well-being. In schools where senior managers are committed you will hear them talking about the concept with passion and often referring to it in their conversations with stakeholders.

Translating personal and professional commitment into a strategic plan

This is a key task for leadership teams. The materials offer senior leadership teams (SLT) a model for devising a strategic plan. A key aspect of the planning process will be to consider how the initiative will be monitored and evaluated, as part of the Plan – Do – Review cycle.

Appointing a coordinator

A coordinator is another 'must have'. Without this person the programme will happen randomly and incoherently and so the potential benefits will be lost. This coordinator must have enough time allowance and resources to undertake a range of tasks. Some of these will be about supporting the culture of emotional health and well-being at work and other tasks will specifically include using the programme and supporting its classroom delivery. (A sample checklist outlining the key role, tasks, qualities and skills is included in Chapter 2.)

One of the first tasks of the coordinator may be to decide on an appropriate taught programme to meet the needs of the school concerned and to present a summary to the SLT for agreement. (Once again a resource sheet is available in Chapter 2 to help with this process.)

Auditing and building on what is already in place and effective

Audits of existing practice and skill levels are invaluable for accelerating the integration of a SEL programme. These identify all the areas of strength that already exist and allow the early steps to be connected to areas that are receptive and ready to change. This means that there are some quick results and gains which can be used to support further development.

There are a number of different types of audit activities that can usefully be carried out, as explained in Chapter 2. Whatever areas of focus are chosen, the key to success is to use the results to ensure that the new initiative meshes with and builds on what is in place and effective already. Such audits can also establish 'baseline' measures which can be used to monitor and evaluate progress if readministered at a later date.

Activities, resources and information are also included in Chapter 2 to enable schools to undertake audits in any of the following areas, with suggestions for structuring and using the feedback obtained effectively:

- mapping current provision in areas linked to SEL

- auditing stakeholders' perceptions of the 'emotional climate'

- finding out what the school does well to support the EHWB of staff and enabling staff to profile their own strengths and areas for development in the key domains of emotional literacy

- finding out how the physical and emotional environment (including adult role-modelling) supports the development of children's SEBS.

Involving stakeholders

The involvement of as many stakeholders as possible in a planned and coherent manner is another critical success factor. Although not a 'new initiative' that has to be incorporated from scratch with all the attendant emotional reactions and overload, introducing a taught SEL curriculum does carry with it the possibility of change. As with anything involving change, the more people who are at least in theoretical agreement with the principles behind it, and also involved with the consultative processes that go with it, the better. That way there will be less opposition, and potential sabotage, later.

Ensuring staff buy in

Staff within a school, who will be centrally involved in delivering and supporting the SEL curriculum both in and out of lesson times, are a key group to have on board from the beginning. If the implementation of the initiative is to be successful it is essential that staff feel valued and listened to. The role of the coordinator is very important in this respect because their approach to the staff will be critical in the on-going success of the programme. Thus approaching the staff with empathy and a willingness to hear responses, both positive and negative, will be a significant feature in the establishment of any programme. If the staff feel valued and listened to in the initial phases, they are more likely to adopt this approach themselves. (Ideas for achieving this are included in the resources and activities in Chapter 2.)

Planning for the on-going maintenance of the programme and for staff development opportunities

Another critical success factor in ensuring that the initiative does not lose both impetus and impact, and that staff remain motivated, is the putting in place of an on-going programme of staff development and support. In most schools, this will take the form of regular staff meetings to develop staff confidence and competence and to allow for joined-up planning and consistency of practice throughout the school.

Because of the nature of the content staff meetings in this area can feel threatening to some teachers, and because of the perceived risk of personal exposure and potential vulnerability it is of the greatest importance that the environment in which the meetings take place feels safe and receptive to different points of view, joint exploration and learning. (Guidelines and ideas for creating such an environment can be found in Chapter 3.)

A further way of providing support for staff which enables them to feel valued and listened to, as well as encouraging good practice in developing children's SEL and increasing capacity within the school, is to implement a system of coaching. Coaching is a powerful development process as it offers an opportunity to personalize the learning and directly apply it to the coachee's work situation. (An outline of a coaching approach can be found in Chapter 3.)

Underlying principles for the effectiveness of work with staff

A learning community

Embedded in a belief based on the importance of social and emotional development in the service of promoting learning is the further belief that learning in itself is important. Thus a school is promoting itself as a community of learners, as well as a community of teachers. The development programme outlined in this book offers a good opportunity for all the staff to learn and develop. They will learn professionally since the delivery of the SEL material calls for particular styles of classroom leadership and they will learn personally because there is allowance for reflection time plus some tools to think about themselves and their own values, feelings, beliefs and situations.

Participation

Along with the culture that supports learning of all kinds and believes in the relevance of personal learning to professional performance is the willingness to participate. Creating an atmosphere where everyone feels not only intellectually willing to engage and participate, but emotionally safe enough to do so, depends greatly on the skill of the coordinator and the ethos of the SLT. In a school where failure is criticized harshly and a judgemental attitude is adopted, emotional safety will be low and participation will be greatly reduced.

However, in a school where the ethos of the leadership team is that failure enhances learning, and where a 'no-blame' approach is taken, emotional safety will be far easier to achieve. Similarly, it will be important for the person responsible to acknowledge and emphasize how much the staff are doing already to achieve SEL development.

Using a solution focused approach

Linked with the positive, no-blame approach to mistakes is the 'solution focused approach'. This means that any discussion becomes forward looking, positive in outlook and concerned only with finding new ways to tackle difficult issues. Participants have a choice about the focus they take; it can be backward looking and regretful, for instance, or forward looking and expectant. If the staff group have 'signed up' to using a solution focused approach, the discussions and activities can always be refocused quickly. The training modules used in this book adopt a solution focused approach throughout and introduce a range of helpful approaches often associated with it.

CHAPTER 2

A Framework for Implementation

The overall framework for implementation is outlined as a stepped process in this chapter and summarized in *Resource 3: Strategic Planning*. The rationale, timing and resources associated with each of the steps outlined in the process are detailed below. It is anticipated that schools will use the framework as a starting point from which to develop their own action plan. The resources for doing so can be found in pages 14–17.

Exploring feasibility. Making the initial commitment

Timing: Two terms prior to implementation of curriculum resource.

Commitment at SLT level is a critical factor for maximizing the success of any initiative (see Chapter 1). In order to make an initial commitment, a critical mass of the SLT will need to consider that they and the school are ready to make the commitment in the context of current demands and opportunities.

Resource 1: School readiness

Resource 2: Resource, readiness, relevance sheet

Strategic planning

Timing: Two terms prior to implementation of curriculum resource.

The demands of the implementation of the whole school SEBS initiative will need to be set against existing demands on school capacity. An awareness of the 'big picture' – the tasks and likely time-scales necessary – enables the SLT to plan strategically and 'ring-fence' the necessary meeting times and resources. This helps to ensure on-going motivation and combats 'initiative fatigue'. It gives a sense of purpose and pace and enables all those involved to see progress. The strategic planning tool (see *Resource 3* pp. 14–17) outlines the key elements that make for a successful initiative. It enables the SLT to record threats and opportunities and also to detail timings, responsibilities and so on.

Resource 3: Strategic planning

Appointing a coordinator

Timing: Two terms prior to implementation of curriculum resource.

This has previously been identified as a critical success factor. In order to ensure an appropriate coordinator is appointed who has the necessary overview, credibility and skill to carry out the key tasks associated with the role, the SLT should consider the general role and skills set described in *Resource 4* (see p. 18) and apply it in their individual context.

Resource 4: The role and skill set of the EL coordinator

Choosing and exploring an appropriate programme

Timing: Two terms prior to implementation of curriculum resource.

It is likely that many primary schools will choose to use SEAL materials (DfES, 2005) or the secondary SEBS materials as and when they become available. Coordinators will need to spend time becoming fully familiar with the resource and be ready to summarize the key points for a range of audiences. Where schools choose to consider other programmes, a useful checklist is included as *Resource 5* (see p. 19).

Resource 5: What to look for in a taught social and emotional curriculum

'Where are we now?' – Exploring current contexts

Timing: One to two terms prior to implementation of curriculum resource.

a) Mapping what is in place already

It is important that the SLT are clear about what is already in place in the organization in order to ensure that the initiative builds on current effective practice, that there is no duplication and that all relevant staff and agencies currently providing support are included in developments. This mapping will enable the SLT to identify and target 'gaps' throughout the initiative.

In order to achieve a comprehensive mapping it is suggested that the coordinator convenes a meeting of a cross section of those adults involved. The group could usefully include: the head; the PSHE coordinator; learning mentors; LSAs; a class teacher and an LEA representative (psychologist, behaviour support teacher and so on).

A useful tool to map provision is the '3 wave' model based on the PNS materials (see *Resource 6* on p. 20). A range of useful questions about current practice is also included.

Resource 6: A sample mapping tool

b) Whole-school emotional health and well-being (EHWB) audits and tools

A quick survey designed to assess the 'emotional temperature' of the school as a whole (based on staff responses) is included (see *Resource 7* on pp. 21–2). The results offer the SLT the opportunity to gain an overview of how EHWB within the school is perceived from a variety of adult perspectives. The second part of the task gives adults the chance to identify the factors within the organization that they find supportive or obstructive to their own EHWB, which will provide a starting point for changes to be made.

It is suggested that staff are also given a copy of *Resource 8* (p. 23) which stresses the importance of 'starting with ourselves' prior to responding to the survey. The completed (anonymous) surveys should be collated and a profile built up which can then be fed back to staff for further discussion.

More in-depth audit and assessment tools at the whole-school level are available both from the DfES (2003) (see for example, *Behaviour and Attendance; Initial and In-depth Audits for Primary Schools*) and commercial suppliers. A useful review of the key available options can be found in Weare's *Developing the Emotionally Literate School*, (2004) (see Chapter 6 of her publication). For more information on tools available see the Appendix to this chapter on page 141.

Resource 7: Whole school emotional temperature gauge – A quick guide

Resource 8: A reading: The importance of starting with ourselves

c) Exploring our own profile of emotional literacy

One of the best ways forward in any setting is to have staff complete an emotional literacy profile. This offers helpful information about one aspect of the baseline state of the setting. It helps to emphasize the importance of starting with the adults in emotional literacy, and can give staff fascinating insights into their own strengths and areas for development.

As staff work through the ten training modules, they will have the opportunity to build up such a profile. Consideration of our own strengths and weaknesses in this area can lead to strong reactions and facilitators and the SLT are advised to follow the guidelines provided within *Resource 9* (pp. 24–5). A personal record sheet is provided as *Resource 10* (p. 26), and a brief interpretation guide as *Resource 11* (p. 27).

Other commercially available profiling tools can offer a more in-depth focus in this area.

Resource   9:   Reading – Undertaking a personal EL profile

Resource 10:   My profile (recording sheet)

Resource 11:   Interpreting the EL profile

d) Exploring the pupil environment

As part of the 'current context' you might like to undertake some exploration of the existing environment, both physical and emotional, within which pupils operate. The reading included as *Resource 12* (pp. 28–9) can be used as a stimulus for staff to reflect on the school and classroom environments.

Much recent guidance from the DfES (*Pedagogy and Practice*, 2004; *PNS (Primary National Strategy): Professional development materials*, 2004a), as well as other national sources of expertise in education and related fields, for example *Promoting Emotional Health and Wellbeing* (NHSS, 2004), have focused on the need to create an environment within schools which offers a supportive climate for learning and development. Both the emotional and physical environments are considered. Many resources are available to enable a more 'formal' exploration of the environment to take place, including the *PNS Behaviour and Attendance In-depth Audit* (DfES, 2003).

Resource 12: The role of the environment in promoting EL

Involving and consulting key stakeholders

Timing: At least one term prior to implementation of curriculum resource.

Involving and consulting key stakeholders at the earliest opportunity has been identified as a critical success factor. For each group relevant to your own context (governors, parents, staff, external agencies, community groups and so on) the EL (Emotional Literacy) coordinator will need to prepare:

- an awareness-raising session

- an opportunity to be consulted and provide feedback

- a follow-up session in which you outline how the feedback has informed the process of implementation

- arrangements for on-going communication and feedback.

The checklist included as *Resource 13* (p. 30) offers a means of planning and recording this process.

Resource 13: Checklist for planning stakeholder awareness, consultation and on-going involvement.

Planning the ongoing staff development programme

Timing: At least one term prior to implementation of curriculum resource.

The staff development programme will need to be planned and agreed at least one term before the agreed SEL programme or curriculum is due to be introduced to the pupils.

Chapter 3 provides guidelines and resources to support the process of planning the staff development programme.

Resource Sheet 1: Whole-school readiness checklist

Please fill in one of the circles in each statement below at the point between the two extremes which you believe represents where the staff group is as a whole.

1 Signed up to do a job of teaching/supporting the delivery of the curriculum?	O O O O O O O O O O	Know and actively share the values expressed in the school mission?
2 More responsive to a pacesetting or controlling style of leadership?	O O O O O O O O O O	More responsive to democratic approaches for involvement and commitment?
3 See mandatory inservice training as the official route to continuing professional development?	O O O O O O O O O O	Operate continuous improvement processes that depend on staff coaching and mentoring as an important part of their development?
4 Emphasize the success of the school as being down to hard work and perseverance?	O O O O O O O O O O	Emphasize the importance of the personal well-being of every individual in the school to the success of the school as a whole?
5 See the curriculum as the most important driver of processes in the school?	O O O O O O O O O O	See the fostering of individuality and creativity within each person in the school to be the driver of the processes within the school?
6 Follow routines and procedures carefully?	O O O O O O O O O O	Innovate and take risks without feeling they will be punished if they fail?
7 Keep school activities within school boundaries?	O O O O O O O O O O	Actively seek links with parents and the community and operate an open door policy?
8 See challenging behaviour as an expression of consciously held resentment and obstinacy?	O O O O O O O O O O	Understand that behaviour is a sometimes unconscious expression of difficult emotional states?
9 Strongly link cognitive intelligence to achievement?	O O O O O O O O O O	Strongly link social and emotional competence to achievement?

Interpretation

The further to the right of the continuum the statements are marked, the more ready the school will be for emotional literacy development. Statements found on the right-hand side of the continuum express the key aspects of a school culture that make it open to change and receptive to an emotionally literate approach. For example, within the school, avoidance of emotional stress is an important activity because stress reduces effectiveness as does excessive evaluation and authoritarianism. On the other hand, self-esteem and personal power development help to reduce stress and improve performance and the quality of relationships. (This sectiion can be seen in the Whole-School Environment Literacy Indicator (Morris and Scott, 2003), published by the School of Emotional Literacy.)

Resource Sheet 2 – Relevance, readiness and resource

Each member of the SLT should note down their individual thoughts on the following factors in relation to the implementation of a whole-school SEL curriculum initiative for discussion.

Relevance

How would implementing an SEL curriculum initiative meet our needs? What would we want it to achieve? How would it fit with current priorities? (Strategic planning tools such as Ofsted action plans and the school improvement plan could usefully be considered at this point.)

Readiness

How ready are we to undertake this? What would need to happen to ensure success? Would things be different at another time?

Resource

What capacity have we got in terms of time, personnel and finance to launch, implement, monitor and evaluate such an initiative? How might it provide a framework for any ongoing or planned initiatives, reduce current demands on capacity?

Adapted from Fullan, 1991

Resource Sheet 3: Strategic planning tool

Key Task	Who? Time needed?	Key outcomes	Threats and opportunities	Agreed action points, deadlines, dates and responsibilities
Exploring feasibility. Making the initial commitment	SLT	■ Decision as to whether to implement now/delay or not to undertake		
Strategic planning	SLT 2 hrs	■ Key tasks are timetabled, time, funding and resources allocated (in the light of current priorities) ■ Monitoring and evaluation systems are considered		
Appointment of a coordinator	SLT 2 hrs	■ An appropriately placed coordinator with a clarity of role and tasks		
Choosing an appropriate taught programme	Coordinator or SLT Research and summarizing — variable period of time	■ An appropriate taught programme is chosen (or devised?) ■ The coordinator is familiar with all aspects of the programme and can summarize these at different levels for a variety of key stakeholders		
Exploring the current context: A Mapping what is in already place	Coordinator of SLT Variable time demands	■ A 'rich picture' of current provision for developing children's SEBS is constructed that shows what, for whom, and how often and the effectiveness of each element has been considered		

▲

Key Task	Who? Time needed?	Key outcomes	Threats and opportunities	Agreed action points, deadlines, dates and responsibilities
B Perceptions of the whole-school 'emotional temperature' **and** Supporting and facilitating factors for staff within the organization		■ The school is aware of staff perceptions of how well it promotes the EHWB of its community and which factors support and obstruct staff's own EHWB ■ The SLT are aware of the specific factors operating within the school that facilitate or hinder staff's EHWB so that changes can be made as appropriate		
C Staff profiles of strengths and vulnerabilities in EL		■ Staff build up a profile of their own strengths and areas of vulnerability in EL and have an opportunity to consider their own professional development in this area within the context of their own situation		
D Exploring the pupil environment	On-going — as part of the development	■ Staff have the opportunity to consider how the school/classroom environment (including their own contribution) might facilitate or obstruct the development of pupils' emotional literacy		

This page can be photocopied. © *Developing Emotionally Literate Staff*, Morris and Casey, 2006

Key Task	Who? Time needed?	Key outcomes	Threats and opportunities	Agreed action points, deadlines, dates and responsibilities
Involving and consulting key stakeholders		■ Key stakeholders will be identified and operational planning arrangements confirmed for ■ an awareness-raising session ■ an opportunity to be consulted and provide feedback ■ a follow-up session in which you outline how the feedback has informed the process of implementation ■ arrangements for on-going communication and feedback Following the awareness/consultation session and feedback ■ each group of stakeholders will know what SEBS are; be familiar with the chosen programme; be aware of the benefits of the EL initiative; how it maps onto the current 'big picture' (as explored in Step 2); what the initiative will 'look like' (as appropriate) ■ key stakeholders will have had an opportunity to voice their thoughts, concerns and suggested roles within the initiative and to feel heard		

Key Task	Who? Time needed?	Key outcomes	Threats and opportunities	Agreed action points, deadlines, dates and responsibilities
Planning the on-going staff development programme		■ the staff development programme is planned and agreed with staff		
The staff development programme will need to be planned and agreed at least one term before the agreed SEL programme or curriculum is due to be introduced to the pupils		■ the 'mix' of training sessions (including key content) and on-going support structures (such as coaching) will be agreed for the following year or appropriate period ■ training sessions will be booked in and allocated the necessary time and resources and roles will be clear		

This page can be photocopied. © *Developing Emotionally Literate Staff*, Morris and Casey, 2006

Resource Sheet 4: The roles and skill set of the emotional literacy coordinator

The emotional literacy coordinator will have a range of roles and tasks, including some or all of the following:

- acting as the key point of contact for, for example, NHSS; cluster groupings; LEA representatives/initiatives; community groups involved in EL

- disseminating information, research and training opportunities from the LEA, DfES, Primary or secondary strategy, outside organizations

- conducting initial audits (EHWB)

- undertaking research into taught EL programmes and feeding this back

- being familiar with the DfES resources available, and able to present summaries to a variety of audiences and stakeholders

- organizing and implementing the structural framework of a school-wide programme

- training new and existing staff

- extending the programme into the home

- creating a team and motivating staff

- managing the administration and interpretation of EL assessments.

Generally the qualities and skills necessary for the role will include:

- personal and professional commitment to the principles and values of emotional literacy and the motivation to further develop his or her skills, knowledge and understanding in the area

- credibility among the staff (being known as an effective practitioner in this area)

- excellent interpersonal skills and good relationships with staff, pupils and parents/carers at all levels

- a strategic overview of current school policy, practice and provision, and the ability to identify the potential for development in this area

- confidence in facilitating staff meetings with a potentially high 'emotional' content and the ability to 'hold' the meeting/training session safely while enabling staff to express a range of experiences and emotions

- confidence and skills in managing the 'dynamics' of the group, and dealing with a range of potential staff responses

- general group leadership skills – setting ground rules, timekeeping, keeping people on task, facilitating groups where necessary, closing the meeting.

Resource Sheet 5: What to look for in a taught social and emotional curriculum

A successful programme

■ Has a whole school focus. This might be expressed through common themes across age groups, joint assemblies, focus weeks and so on. The importance of congruence between the environment and the 'taught' aspect will be made clear.

■ Is explicit. A 'taught' SEL curriculum makes social and emotional learning the explicit and specific subject matter for sessions.

■ Is clear about what it is aiming to develop. It includes an appropriate range of learning intentions with the intention that these can be shared with pupils and worded so that they can know if they have been successful.

■ Is spiral. The nature and depth of social and emotional understanding changes over time and with experience. Also, effective behaviours vary according to age — what is accepted in a seven-year-old may not be appropriate in a fifteen-year-old. There is therefore an inbuilt need to revisit subject matter regularly. SEL programmes need to allow for the regular revisiting of key areas, offering the opportunity to build on the skills that have been acquired previously using activities and resources at an age, or developmentally appropriate, level.

■ Uses a range of teaching and learning styles. A range of teaching strategies should be used, particularly those that are participative and experiential, to ensure that different learning styles and pupils with a range of intelligences, personal, cultural and experiential histories are included and engaged.

■ Recognizes the effect of culture- and gender-based differences. These may affect pupils' motivation and comfort levels with the activities presented in the resource and will need to be considered by staff. For example, certain cultures regard direct eye contact between a young person and a more senior member of society as extremely ill-mannered. Pupils need to know that it is safe and appropriate (indeed valuable) to say, 'in my home we do/did it this way...', or 'if I did that, my parents would think...' Within a safe environment that values and celebrates cultural diversity, it is important that teachers find ways of finding out where differences lie, and model interest and respect accordingly.

■ Allows for skills to be practised, reinforced and generalized. Pupils need to practise newly acquired skills, firstly in a safe, managed environment with the teacher or adult in the role of 'coach', and then increasingly independently.

Resource Sheet 6: A sample 'provision mapping' format

ENVIRONMENTAL FACTORS THAT IMPACT INDIRECTLY ON PUPILS e.g. whole school staff training on behaviour/management			ENVIRONMENTAL FACTORS THAT IMPACT INDIRECTLY ON PUPILS e.g. staff support mechanisms
	Wave 1 support representsany intervention that all children can or do benefit from.	Examples might include: A taught 'SEL' curriculum; PSHE; circle time; RE; assemblies; school council. breakfast clubs, NHSS.	
	Wave 2 support represents any intervention that some children benefit from.	Examples might include: Small group support to help pupils develop their social skills or anger management skills, peer mediation training.	
	Wave 3 support represents any intervention that only a few children might benefit from. (NB: Children are likely to have multi-agency support.)	Examples might include: Support from Child and Adolescent Mental Health teams; support from an educational psychologist or behaviour support teacher or learning mentor.	

Key questions to ask:

What key knowledge, skills and understanding do pupils develop through these activities?

How effective are these interventions in achieving such development?

How suitable are the teaching methods we use in developing a pupil's SEL?

How is progress meaured? How are pupils involved in the process of measuring progress?

What do we do really well? What could we do differently?

Where are the gaps?

Resource Sheet 7: Whole-school emotional temperature gauge – a quick guide

Please indicate your agreement with the statement, and make any comments.

4 = strongly agree; 3 = mostly agree; 2 = mostly disagree; 1 = strongly disagree.

You can complete the 'thermometer reading' below to see how highly you rate the school ethos (the 'hotter' it is, the better it is likely to support the EHWB of stakeholders). Sheets can be given in and collated for overall temperature.

	4	3	2	1	Comments
1 I feel empowered and motivated by the school management					
2 My views and expertise are sought out and valued					
3 I feel able to express my opinions even if they may lead to disagreements					
4 I believe that my emotional health and well-being are important to the school					
5 I feel able to risk making a mistake – this would be seen as part of the learning process					
6 Relationships are generally good between pupils					
7 Relationships are generally good between staff and pupils					
8 Relationships between parents and staff are generally good					
9 Relationships among the staff are generally good					
10 The values and beliefs of the school include the importance of promoting social and emotional learning					
11 I believe that most staff share the school's beliefs and values					
12 Pupils are supported in developing self-direction and responsibility for their learning and behaviour					
13 The school environment is welcoming to all, celebrating cultural diversity					

This page can be photocopied. © *Developing Emotionally Literate Staff*, Morris and Casey, 2006

	4	3	2	1	Comments
14 Adults model the behaviours they encourage in pupils (e.g. respect, fairness)					
15 Pupils feel safe in the classroom					
16 Pupils feel safe in school					
17 Pupils feel able to approach staff when they need support					

On the back of this sheet, please divide the page into two columns headed 'supportive aspects' and 'obstructive aspects' and list the factors within school that support or obstruct your own feelings of emotional well-being.

Resource Sheet 8: Reading

The importance of 'starting with ourselves'

The emotional health and well-being of everyone in a school community are so important that several audits have been developed by organizations committed to the development of emotional literacy. These audits explore, through confidential questionnaires, which areas of the setting support and which might hinder the development of social and emotional learning in staff and pupils. They also give everyone a chance to detail what changes might be helpful.

Whilst EL, in its early days of development, tended to focus on target groups with specific needs and thus be underpinned by a deficit model of defining the problem (support would be forthcoming only when something was already 'wrong'), it has become vitally important that this has been balanced with the development and support of positive mental and emotional health. The latter implies a perspective where human strength and health are assumed to be the norm, rather than believing that there will always be deficits in emotional and social health. From this positive perspective we would look at what is supportive and strong already. We would then think about how we could build from these points. This dual focus in emotional literacy is very important – as well as looking for ways to work remedially, we must make sure that we value and pay attention to positive emotional health and well-being.

Mental health and emotional well-being depend on a variety of circumstances, all acting in concert. For example, a person's optimistic attitude combined with a good balance between home and work lives, together with an absence of chronic ill-health plus good working conditions where social, professional and emotional needs are met within a supportive physical environment, all make for an emotionally healthy person. That individual may still have some areas of self-awareness they could develop, or some strategies for managing relationships more effectively which they could learn, but they would find that quite easy given their positive everyday state. At least half of the input to emotional health and well-being is to do with personal attitudes and the ability to create a life that takes all the needs of one's personality into account. A significant number of conditions that surround emotional health and well-being are related to the work setting. It is, therefore, worth paying a great deal of attention to this area as often there are things that we can change relatively easily. The provision of a socially and emotionally supportive workplace can have a dramatic effect on staff morale and attitude.

Resource Sheet 9: Reading – undertaking a personal EL profile

The risks and benefits

This information can make a big difference to the success or difficulty we experience in implementing the initiative. Knowing our own strengths and weaknesses makes it far easier to work with children and young people, not to mention colleagues and family! Our self-awareness is greater and our confidence in our own ability to work in this way is increased. Even if we are not as strong on some of the scales as we would like to be, undertaking a profiling exercise gives the opportunity to develop those aspects, especially if workplace coaching is available. Being prepared to experiment with using a personal profile already shows strength in the areas of openness and flexibility, which are aspects students need to have too.

The Emotional Literacy and Resilience Profile

The purpose of the profile is to help you reflect on your own current abilities and areas for development in the key domains of emotional literacy and resilience: remember that this is a 'snapshot' – our ability to deploy the skills we have is context dependent and hangs on our overall life stressors and satisfactions, the environment in which we are operating and immediate factors such as tiredness, illness and so on.

The profile has been developed to be a self-help tool only. It is not designed so that you can compare yourself with others or against a standard score which indicates a 'norm' – it is purely a tool for you to use to reflect on your own skills, and to have as a helpful self-comparison when done at different times of your life or even on an annual basis. It can be shared with others or not. The choice is entirely within your control. We do recommend, however, that you share it with one other person if you feel comfortable with this as it is particularly effective when shared with a coach, critical friend or 'buddy'. For many of us it can seem as if nothing is different and at times we may feel despondent. A coach, on the other hand, will easily remember the situation as it was and see positive moves where we cannot. Having this 'touchstone' is enormously helpful. Anyone who sees the results and who forms a part of on-going development work should also agree to keep the information confidential (with the standard provisos). This is not just good professional practice; it is critical for establishing the sense of security and trust upon which all work on our own emotional literacy depends.

Having completed all the modules you will have rated your strengths and areas of vulnerability in the key domains of emotional literacy: – self-awareness, self-management, motivation and resilience, awareness of others (empathy) and relationship management.

Completing your Emotional Literacy Profile

As you work your way through the training modules, you will be given undisturbed time for finishing the various aspects of the questionnaire. You will be asked to complete each scale by circling the number (3,2,1,0) in the column which best describes your response to each statement or question. Work quickly and stick to your initial response. Try to be as honest with yourself as possible and remember that only you will see your answers. If you have trouble answering a question, think of how a friend or co-worker might rate you on that item.

Finding your score

After completing each scale, add up the value of the numbers you have circled in each vertical column. Place that total at the bottom of each column. Add the bottom row totals together to get your score for that scale. Write that total in the square provided. Next to the scale there is a ruler with six levels. Your score will fall within the range on one of these six levels. Fill in the triangle that corresponds to your score.

Once you have finished the profile you can transfer your scores onto the score card (see Resource 10). After marking the corresponding triangles on the score card, you will then be able to join them up as illustrated and see at a glance the 'picture' of your profile as it is right now. The Emotional Resilience Profile Interpretation Guide will help you to understand your scores.

Resource Sheet 10: My profile

Guidance on interpreting this profile is to be found in Resource 11 following

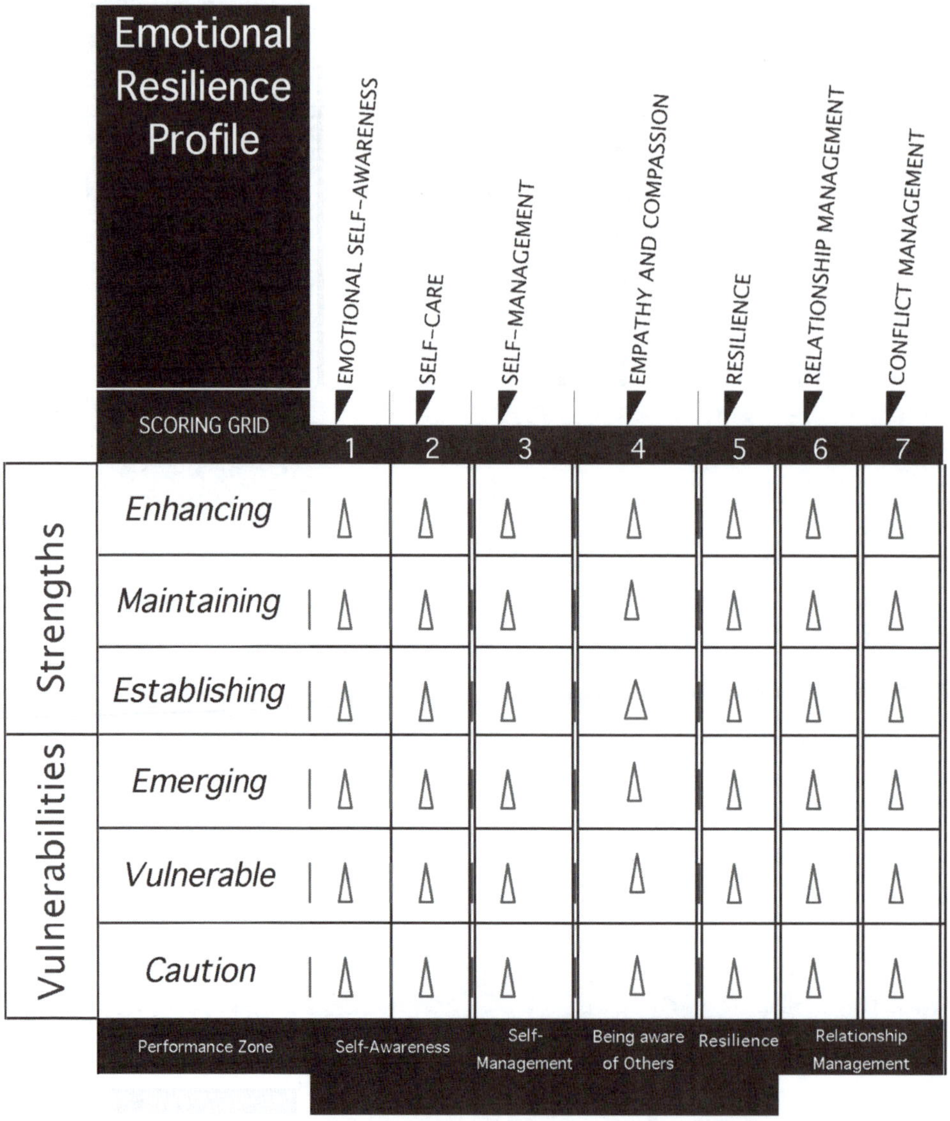

Emotional Resilience Profile

Column headings:
1. EMOTIONAL SELF-AWARENESS
2. SELF-CARE
3. SELF-MANAGEMENT
4. EMPATHY AND COMPASSION
5. RESILIENCE
6. RELATIONSHIP MANAGEMENT
7. CONFLICT MANAGEMENT

SCORING GRID		1	2	3	4	5	6	7
Strengths	Enhancing	Δ	Δ	Δ	Δ	Δ	Δ	Δ
	Maintaining	Δ	Δ	Δ	Δ	Δ	Δ	Δ
	Establishing	Δ	Δ	Δ	Δ	Δ	Δ	Δ
Vulnerabilities	Emerging	Δ	Δ	Δ	Δ	Δ	Δ	Δ
	Vulnerable	Δ	Δ	Δ	Δ	Δ	Δ	Δ
	Caution	Δ	Δ	Δ	Δ	Δ	Δ	Δ

Performance Zone | Self-Awareness | Self-Management | Being aware of Others | Resilience | Relationship Management

Resource Sheet 11: Interpreting the EL profile (see Resource Sheet 10)

A definition of each key area in which you are invited to construct a profile will be provided as you undertake the 'personal profiling' activity within the relevant modules. This resource outlines the significance of each score 'band', and should be brought to each development session.

The score 'bands' can be interpreted as follows:

Enhancing: A score at this level is helping to make you feel good and get results.

Maintaining: A score at this level means that this aspect of your emotional literacy is helping you maintain a proficient, well-balanced output.

Establishing: This level of score means that either you are developing positively in this area of your emotional literacy, or that you are feeling less proficient in this area compared to previously. You need to recognize the direction of the trend – is it up or down compared to say one year ago?

Emerging: Hopefully this level of score indicates that you have been vulnerable but are now beginning to strengthen in this area. There is enough energy and ability here for you to grow and develop. To gain more quality of life you need to focus on this area.

Vulnerable: A score at this level means that you are probably experiencing a lot of stress and pressure which are affecting this aspect of your emotional literacy. Take this score as a warning signal that this area needs and deserves more of your attention.

Caution: An EL score at this level is certainly sending a danger signal to you. Scores here often impact on our resilience and performance and affect our health. Please give this your attention by focusing on it with the help of those who you feel will support you.

Resource Sheet 12: Reading – the key role of the environment in EL

Two of the biggest impacts on the development of children's skills in emotional literacy are the depth and richness of the emotional environment and the variety and forethought that have gone into the physical environment.

Creating an enriched emotional environment

Creating a safe place to talk, listen and learn takes time and effort from everyone. Adults have to set up the conditions where trust can flourish. Seeing mistakes as learning opportunities gives students permission to get it wrong without feeling as if they themselves are bad. Adults need to create an atmosphere of safety through an attitude of respect and interest.

Small interactions between adults and students make a big difference to the emotional environment. From smiling and being engaged as they come through the door, to the use of their names as you say goodbye, the day is full of opportunities to connect, deepen relationships and to model and develop social, emotional and behavioural skills and learning.

Even as professional skilled adults, our ability to deploy our social and emotional skills varies on a continuum from sophistication to incompetence depending on context. In a new environment, in situations in which we feel threatened or disliked, in times of stress, exhaustion and uncertainty, even the most emotionally literate adult can find themselves behaving in the most emotionally illiterate ways! In a school context this can have significant consequences, so as one anonymous quote puts it:

> Don't worry that you do not think the children are listening to you; worry that they are watching everything you do.

Staff who hold attitudes of empathy, respect, openness and optimism create a fertile environment for students to easily absorb much of the social, emotional and behavioural learning they will require.

The physical environment

Like the enriched emotional environment, the physical environment plays a significant part in developing the brain and supporting learning. Often small changes that we make to the physical environment can improve learning and development substantially. Students all have different environmental preferences for how and where they learn most effectively, but it is possible to consider some general guidelines that will support the learning of the majority.

In **Behaviour and Attendance – In-depth primary audit** (DfES, 2003) the following descriptors are included on the subject of the environment. How true are they of your school?

The school as a whole:
- the external environment is safe, attractive and well maintained
- the external environment is resourced to encourage the behaviours expected of children (for example, attractive and varied recreational spaces, adequate litter bins, water fountains)
- inside the school, the environment is safe, attractive and well maintained and reflects children's interests and achievements
- the school environment is welcoming to all, and celebrates the cultural diversity of our society and the individuals within it

2 ■ A FRAMEWORK FOR IMPLEMENTATION

- in-class resources are adequate for meeting the needs of the children and ensuring that everyone is included

- there is adequate supervision so that children feel safe and free to move around at breaktimes, lunchtimes, before and after school

- clubs and activities are provided to engage children in a range of interests and these help to support positive behaviours, develop children's SEBS and promote regular attendance

- quiet places are provided where children can talk or read at breaktimes and lunchtimes.

In the classroom:

The following guidelines, developed by one of the authors, highlight some additional areas of focus. These elements impact on children's feelings of safety and security, their ability to engage actively with learning and also to behave appropriately:

- space (sufficient for purpose)

- presentation (attractive and selective; changed regularly; wall space used for displays which are interactive, demonstrate the value placed on children's work and celebrate cultural diversity)

- noise (everything audible that should be)

- lighting (reasonable/everyone can see without difficulty: there is a choice of places to sit in brighter or more subdued lighting depending on learning preference, and there is little or no fluorescent lighting with daylight spectrum light available and used when possible

- temperature (within working range 66–74F (20–23C)

- smell (pleasantly scented for learning)

- seating arrangement (flexible; suitable and appropriately arranged furniture for nature of tasks; chalkboard/whiteboard easily seen by all)

- ease of movement around room (resources for pupils accessible; appropriate storage for children's belongings; movement space)

- Multiple Intelligence learning styles areas to encourage subject learning in a variety of ways (visual and tactile representations)

- access to water for drinking.

Resource Sheet 13: Checklist for planning stakeholder awareness, consultation and ongoing involvement

Stakeholder Group (Name)	Group 1	Group 2	Group 3
Awareness session date and time			
What is the initiative about?			
What are SEAL/SEBS/SEL ?			
Rationale for including in curriculum			
Outline of the programme (including timescale)			
Links to other initiatives, subject areas and aspects of school life			
Time and resource implications for the school			
What information and input will other groups have (e.g. training for staff; information and input for parents/governors/pupils etc.)?			
Other:			
Arrangements for consultation (format/dates/deadlines)			
Arrangements for feedback following consultations (format/dates/deadlines)			
Arrangements for on-going communication			
Other			

PART 2 THE STAFF PROFESSIONAL DEVELOPMENT PROGRAMME

CHAPTER 3

Setting Up a Staff Development Programme

Key principles

The involvement of all adults

Because the success of 'taught' SEL programmes depends so crucially on the 'caught' dimension – the environment within which skills knowledge and understandings will be 'tried out' and consolidated, and on the ethos within which these efforts will be received – it is particularly important that, wherever possible, *all* adults within an organization are involved in the development programme to the appropriate degree. The key role of adult modelling and support was discussed earlier in *Resource 12* in Chapter 2). This includes caretaking and administrative staff, teaching and non-teaching staff – all of whom have a role to play in shaping the ethos of the organization, and creating a safe and supportive 'learners' environment'.

The need for a safe environment

Fostering our abilities to support the development of children's skills in the area of social and emotional learning is inherently different to developing our skills in many other subject areas.

- although we are developing our professional skills, the content area requires us to consider here our own skills and abilities, in a way that learning a new method of teaching addition or subtraction may not

- we may fear that vulnerabilities in our own lives may be exposed

- we might worry that our own feelings may get 'out of hand'

- we could believe that we do not have adequate skills in this area

- we may be unwilling to take a risk, or go against the prevailing consensus.

Because of the nature of the subject matter, it is important that the group establish a safe environment in which open and honest discussion can take place in the sessions related to this area. Often schools consider this in relation to pupils, but fail to do so in relation to the learning that adults do together. Module 1 offers an opportunity for adults to consider their needs, ground rules and to establish the conditions in which trust can be established.

Many schools have found a 'buddying' system useful to establish structure and safety. Each staff member chooses a 'buddy', and if at any point they wish to leave the session for some time-out, it is understood that their 'buddy' will follow them to check if support is required and offer this if needed. Similarly at the end of the session, if issues have been left unresolved for an individual, they will know that their 'buddy' can be available for support.

Engaging the heart and the head

Because social and emotional learning requires the engagement of the heart *and* the head, particular types of learning opportunities are more helpful than others. In particular, it is more effective to experience than be told: social and emotional learning is more effective when we have the opportunity to link it to our own experiences and before we try to work at pupil level. We need to have an opportunity to question and interact, participate and share thoughts and feelings, in order to help connect that knowledge to what we know already and thus 'shape' our learning.

This programme builds on research findings about effective CPD, which suggest that this is the outcome when it is collaborative (that is, the whole staff learning together) and on-going over a period of time.

TIP: Many schools have suggested that it is important in such a programme to provide a folder (and dividers and so on) for each participant, to ensure that the various handouts and resources can be kept together.

Elements of the staff meeting – a suggested structure and some ideas for effective practice

The following suggested structure assumes a staff meeting of 1 hour and 30 minutes, and includes all of the following recommended elements:

- an opportunity to feedback on the pre-session/intersessional activity

- a starter activity

- the content of one training module

- an opportunity for action planning/agreeing an intersessional activity

- a closing activity.

It is suggested that the learning from the staff meeting is supported and embedded through

- the 'intersessional activity' (see below)

- an optional and personal learning log (see *Resource 3.2* on p. 38)

- a coaching session where possible (*see Resource 3.3* on p. 39)

Each of these elements is considered in the following sections of this chapter.

Planning the session

Some organizations have used the following strategies to get meetings off to a good start:

- making sure that staff physiological needs are met (providing refreshments and comfort, ensuring the room temperature is OK)

- holding the session in a different room to 'normal' staff meetings

- using a 'circle time' approach where everyone has eye contact with everyone else

- allowing staff one minute to 'empty their minds' (for example, by writing down what they have to do afterwards to prevent dwelling on outstanding issues, or 'checking in' with a buddy) and then refocus.

Pre-session tasks

Pre-session tasks are provided for each Module. They serve to 'tune in' participants to the key areas of the session, and to enable some forethought to be given to the subject matter, with an opportunity for questions, examples, issues to be articulated. They also ensure some degree of 'common knowledge'. Participants may like to discuss the importance of this in Module 1 – many schools have 'signed up' to doing the task and have established the importance for a group of each individual taking the responsibility for doing so.

Ground rules

Module 1 offers the opportunity for staff to agree these together. They provide clarity and safety in terms of expectations, and contribute to the development of a trusting ethos. Because they are agreed by the group, they also provide a 'reference point' against which the behaviour of individuals can be held to account without the need for personal recrimination. The ground rules can, of course, be revisited as often as necessary and should be displayed in the staffroom. Some schools have gone further and produced a joint 'policy' for how adults will work together (see for example, *Resource 3.1* on p. 37).

Starter activity

Many schools use a participative, active, fun 'starter activity' to generate energy and facilitate a positive mind-set prior to the session. Circle time games and activities offer a broad range of possibilities. If you are in a foundation stage or primary setting using the SEAL materials (DfES, 2005), there are a range of activities that could be adapted for the staff meeting.

Learning intentions

As with pupils, it is important to be clear about what the session aims to achieve. Learning intentions are included for all Modules. An appropriate 'closing' activity (see below) is often to review the extent to which these intentions have been met for individuals.

Learning opportunities/activities

The following ideas are suggested to sustain motivation and enthusiasm:

- use a variety of stimuli to link to different learning styles and intelligences

- engage participants at the adult level, before considering the issues of working with pupils

- offer participants the opportunity to change partners by using 'mix-up' games (for example, all those with brown shoes/earrings/a child over ten change places)

- recognize contributions – make people feel that they matter

- as a facilitator: 'walk the talk', act as a model of the values you are espousing.

Applications and action planning

Suggest that participants throughout the session note down ways in which the learning might impact on their practice – for example, things they might do differently, try out and so on. Alternatively, offer participants five minutes or so at the end of the session for reflection and the recording of any practical steps they will take as a result of the session. A pro-forma is provided for this purpose (see *Resource 3.4* on p. 41).

Closing activity

Because of the nature of the subject matter and its potential emotional impact, it is important to provide an opportunity for staff to experience closure and an opportunity to 'move on' from the session. Good ways to achieve this include: a simple 'round' (for example, One thing I have enjoyed/learned/will change as a result of this session is ...), or 'check-out' time with a partner (maybe their respective 'buddy' if you are using this system), or a chance to finish on a positive note by acknowledging something that someone in the group has done that you liked/found supportive/respected, and so on.

Reflective learning log

Participants might be offered the chance to keep such a log over the course of the sessions, useful whether as a support to them in reflecting on personal progress, to share with a trusted 'buddy', coach or colleague, or to use as the basis for a personal action plan. See *Resource 3.2* on p. 38.

Intersessional activity

The most effective models of CPD all seem to include an element of 'trying out new learning'. The intersessional activities we have outlined offer an opportunity for participants to do just this. They suggest, for example, considering this within a coaching context, or within the reflective learning log, or at the next Module session.

Resource Sheet 3.1: A policy for staff communication and conduct

Rationale

At 'X' Primary School we value all members of the school community. We believe that teamwork is important and valuable, and that what a team can achieve together is much more than the sum of what each individual member can achieve. We aspire to demonstrate these values in all our daily interactions.

Purposes

- to establish systems of communication which enable every staff member to feel that they have a voice and are listened to

- to establish effective systems of communication which enable the school to run smoothly and which facilitate the work of all members of the school community

- to establish ways of interacting which create harmony in the school and which make working in Cameley a pleasant experience

- to create a happy working environment where each member of the community feels valued and supported

- to nurture a positive ethos in the school, which will enable all staff to give of their best and which will support well-being.

Guidelines

- staff treat each other in an open, honest way

- we treat each other with respect and consideration at all times

- we aim to resolve any disagreements or concerns as swiftly as possible

- we assume the best of our colleagues, and try not to be over-critical

- we always try to speak directly to the person whose behaviour has caused upset and to do this as quickly as possible. No 'festering'!

- if it is not possible to follow the above guideline for some reason, then we go to a senior manager — preferably the head, and discuss with her ways of resolving the upset as soon as possible

- we aim to always speak positively about each other, and about pupils and parents

- if at all possible we avoid non-specific criticism

- if a colleague is feeling upset or is in need of support, we try to find time to listen and we offer help gently, for example ' Would it be any help if …?' or 'What could we do that would help you?'

- we acknowledge each other's kindnesses, suggestions or support with thanks

- we try to be each other's Positive Wizards (self-esteem building team) as frequently as possible

With thanks to Chris Lindup

Resource Sheet 3.2: Reflective learning log and action planning

Date

Significant experience or learning

What happened ?   (… activity – process – constraints …)

Why ?

Conclusions   (…outcome – lessons learned…)

Actions   (…plans to do something better/different…)

When?

This page can be photocopied. © *Developing Emotionally Literate Staff*, Morris and Casey, 2006

Resource Sheet 3.3: Guidelines on setting up a coaching programme

The key characteristic of a coaching programme is that each person receives individualized help and support from somebody whose input they value, in a confidential and solution-focused approach. It is important that the process models the methodology for working in this area with pupils. Coaching is a process of development that takes place within a relationship of trust and consists of a series of meetings and discussions where the focus is on an activity, behaviour or process agreed with the coachee (the focus is likely to be on the intersessional activity currently being undertaken). The aim of coaching is to help unlock a person's potential to maximize their own performance. It is about assisting them to learn – rather than teaching them from an expert point of view. Thus the focus is very positive, with strong expectations that the coachee will achieve what they want to achieve. The focus is strongly on 'how' things happened, rather than 'what' happened.

What are the qualities of a good coach?

- can empower the coachee through a balance of support and challenge

- has the ability to build and maintain trust and rapport with the coachee and coach will always act reliably and professionally

- maintains good control of their own emotions, moods and energies

- conveys an attitude of non-judgementalism

- is enabling of coachee to find their own answers

- acts in a supportive way to help the coachee to become aware of their emotions, moods and energies

- is able to pay attention to a wide range of information: social, personal and professional

- is skillful enough to listen actively and question effectively.

The COACH model as a useful tool for planning and reviewing what might take place in a coaching session

C urrent reality check – the coach and coachee will discuss what is happening now. This acts as a baseline, or comparison with the previous meeting.

O bjectives for the session – together the two will develop their aims for that particular session. Typically the coach will ask the coachee 'What do you want to achieve today?' This will then be discussed to check if it is realistic and in line with the overall goals for the sessions.

A ctions and options – in the middle section of a session the focus will be on looking at the 'how' of actions and activities by the coachee that have produced good results. They will also, typically, focus on the 'how' of what did not go so well. This helps the coachee really understand the reasons for the difference in results.

C ommitment to action – towards the end of a session the coach and coachee will refine and define the coachee's next set of actions. These are usually some behaviours or trials that the coachee commits to practising or trying over the next period of time.

H ow did it go review – once again a very short review typically takes place at the end of a session where the coach and coachee check back to the objective/s given by the coachee at the start. The extent to which these have been met, or the significance of any deviation from the objectives, gives important information for further development to both parties.

▶

Coaching Approach

Coaches adopt a particular strategy for development work. They operate cooperatively with their coachees and do not adopt an attitude of expertise. They hold firm beliefs about the innate capability of others and, whilst open to giving direct guidance when it comes to skills that are to be learnt, they hold back from strong direction in other areas. This enables the coachee to thoroughly experience the learning for themselves and to form their own conclusions about the experience. Thus a coach will always form a mutual agreement about goals and objectives, give honest and direct feedback, help the coachee to develop their personal skills and solve their own problems, support them in developing an action plan and review their own and the coachee's performance and progress together.

Resource Sheet 3.4: Action planning

Individual post-session action planning   Date:

Intersessional focus:

Link to Module learning :

What will I do?

When will I do it?

What outcomes am I looking for?
(How will I know if the focus has made a difference?)

How will I record/feedback these?

My next three steps to make it happen

1

2

3

CHAPTER 4

The Mix and Match Modules

This chapter provides a comprehensive series of learning modules to help staff become familiar with the concept of emotional literacy. They also promote the use of resource materials connected with its development within the school and enable staff to become confident and competent in its use. The modules can be used in staff meetings, or in specially allocated time slots and are facilitated by the emotional literacy coordinator. We suggest that the modules are used in the order they are written as there is an internal logic to the sequence of learning. However it is also possible to pick and mix in ways that suit the areas for focus and the preferences of the staff group. One of the most important principles of emotional literacy is that there is no 'off the shelf' solution for any aspect of its development. Each solution must come about through discussion and understanding of the individual needs of the people, the group and the community as a whole. Thus the coordinator when planning the training sessions will make sure that they have a clear understanding of the needs, preferences and priorities of the members.

The modules are laid out using a clear template to help the planning process. This template includes suggested timing during the year for using each module in order to support an integrative and effective whole school approach. There are also aims and learning intentions, a resource list and material for each module, mention of links to other initiatives and resources, facilitator's notes and a range of activities for exploring each particular focus. There are also addition suggestions for intersessional work which will help to make the training programme extremely effective if they are used. Start by reading through the titles of the modules and the learning intentions to gain a good overall understanding of the potential and possibilities within this section, then feel free to adapt and adopt as fits your setting's situation.

Module 1: Creating a learning environment: feeling valued, included and empowered

Suggested timing of session: June/July Year 1

Aims and learning intentions

Staff will

- understand the importance of having an environment for learning which helps us to feel valued, included and empowered

- be familiar with Maslow's Hierarchy of Needs (see Resource Sheet 1) and its importance in helping us to understand what needs must be met before learning can take place

- be familiar with the three components of self -esteem and how the environment needs to develop and support them if learning is to take place

- apply this understanding to both adult and pupil contexts for learning

- Understand the importance of, and have the skills to use, active listening techniques.

Underpinning concepts and theory

- Maslow's Hierarchy of Needs

- components of self-esteem

- active listening.

Resources

- Resource Sheet 1: Maslow's Hierarchy of Needs

- Resource Sheet 2: A model of self-esteem

Links to DfES primary SEAL materials

Key outcomes in all themes of the DfES SEAL curriculum materials include:

- valuing ourselves and others

- exploring and valuing diversity

- creating an environment in which all feel included and safe

- participating

- taking personal responsibility for learning and behaviour.

Theme 1 includes the opportunity for each class to contribute to a class charter, which sets out the sort of environment pupils would like, and how each can contribute to it.

Suggested activities – facilitator's notes

Maslow's hierarchy   5 minutes

Give out *Resource Sheet 1: Maslow's Hierarchy of Needs* and talk through the key points.

Key points

- In both adult and pupil contexts, learning will not take place unless certain preconditions are met. Maslow, a humanist psychologist in the 1950s, provided us with a model of what these pre-conditions might be.

- He drew up what he considered to be a universal 'hierarchy of human needs'. This proposed that we as humans would not be motivated by a higher need unless our 'lower' needs (from the hierarchy) were met. For example, we know from our own experiences that it is difficult to focus on new information or learning if we are hungry, too hot, feeling unsafe or insecure. Equally, we are not likely to be motivated to learn if we feel alienated – that we do not belong or that we are not valued within a group.

- In Maslow's terms the lower needs have to be satisfied before we will be motivated by learning opportunities and intellectual curiosity. This applies to adults as much as pupils.

- Ask participants to reflect for a minute or so, or to talk in pairs, about a time when they may have experienced trying to learn or achieve an objective in a hostile environment – where they felt disliked, for example, or that others did not value them. Take brief feedback.

- Maslow's Hierarchy suggests that we will not learn well if we do not value ourselves as individuals. The learning environment must support and develop our self-esteem if we are to learn well.

Self-esteem   10 minutes

Give out *Resource Sheet 2: The components of self-esteem*, (Morris, 2001) and talk through the key points:

Key points:

- The model consists of three components: our sense of acceptable self; our sense of 'belonging'; our sense of personal power (a sense of our own power to make an impact and influence events).

- We learn best when the environment supports all three components of self-esteem. Having sound self-esteem means that we value ourselves and relies on the three components listed above.

- Point out the similarities between this and Maslow's model. Both, for example, emphasize that the need to belong and to value ourselves must be satisfied before we can fully access learning opportunities.

- Emphasize the importance of the adult/pupil relationship in establishing a sense of 'belonging'. The language we use and the way we speak to a pupil tells the child the extent to which they are valued and belong in that classroom. Ask staff to guess how much of a 'message' is received by the listener through the words we use, the way we say the words, our body language (the respective answers are 7 per cent; 38 per cent and 55 per cent). Reflect together on the implications of this for the messages we communicate to pupils.

- This model of self-esteem also suggests that, in addition to the preconditions for learning proposed by Maslow, the environment needs to provide us with opportunities to feel that we have some control or power over events. This translates broadly into our need to feel that our ideas are being heard and acted upon.

The following activities ask staff to reflect on how the 'preconditions' for learning (including support for our self-esteem) are met for them in staff meetings, and also how these are experienced by pupils within the school and classroom.

ACTIVITY 1.1: Application to adult contexts	**15 minutes**

Introduce the idea that developing our abilities to support the development of pupil skill in the area of social and emotional learning is inherently different from developing our skills in many other subject areas.

Ask participants to offer ideas on what these differences might be and on how they might affect us. Some ideas are included in the introduction to Chapter 3.

Because of the nature of the subject matter, it is important that we as staff establish a safe environment for open and honest discussion in the sessions related to this area.

In pairs or small groups, ask staff to consider and record on a flipchart the factors that would promote a 'safe' environment in which individuals feel valued, included and empowered, and in which honest and open discussion and joint exploration in inset/staff meetings can take place with any factors that might hinder this process, drawing on Maslow's Hierarchy and the components of self-esteem where appropriate.

Take feedback from this activity, and having shared the perceptions, ask the group to agree a set of ground rules for future sessions. These can be written up and displayed.

ACTIVITY 1.2: Application to pupil contexts   **10 minutes**

Ask participants to discuss in pairs or small groups what they would do to create a classroom/school in which pupils' needs to belong, to feel valued and to feel empowered are met. Ask them to feed back under the following headings:

How, in the school or classroom, do we help meet pupils':

■ physiological needs?

■ needs for safety (physical and emotional)?

■ need to belong?

■ need to know and value themselves as individuals?

■ need to have opportunities to contribute and influence (self-efficacy)?

■ need to come to know and understand themselves?

If not volunteered, you might like to add the following factors which can help promote a sense of safety and enable trust to be built up over time:

■ predictability

■ understanding of purpose – shared objectives

■ clear parameters – knowing what is acceptable and what is not, and having clarity about the consequences.

ACTIVITY 1.3: Active listening skills   **20 minutes**

Key points

■ One key strategy in helping to ensure that individuals feel valued is using the skill of 'active' or 'empathic' listening. It is important that all staff experience this at an adult level, if they are to understand its importance when working with pupils. This activity aims to enable staff to understand the importance of this key professional skill.

■ 'Active' or 'empathic' listening takes adults beyond the everyday experience of listening – it involves paying close attention and really focusing to make sense of what is being said and its meaning for the speaker. We need to empty ourselves of those things that are concerning us at that particular moment, put aside any personal emotions and have an open, non-judgemental mind. During listening time like this the aim is to discover, not to correct or give advice.

Ask participants to think of something in their life that they might find it difficult to talk about. (No-one will be asked to speak about this.) Ask them to look around the group and see if there's anyone there that they might choose to talk with about this kind of thing. (Again, no-one will be asked to reveal the name of this person.) If there is no-one within the group, ask them to think of someone else that they know.

Ask them to think about why they chose this particular person, what qualities they think they have that made them choose them. Take feedback on these qualities and flipchart them. These are the qualities of the good listener.

▶

47

ACTIVITY 1.3: *Continued*

Ask participants to get into pairs and divide each pair into As and Bs. The former leave the room and think of something that is important to them or that they feel excited about – tell them that directly afterwards they are going to talk to their partner for one minute about it.

Inside the room the Bs are told to do everything they can to show their partner that they are not interested. Get them to suggest what bad listeners do. Divide a flipchart sheet in two vertically and write this list in the left-hand column. The list might include:

- lack of eye contact
- shuffling papers
- interrupting
- asking lots of questions
- making judgements ('Well, that wasn't very sensible was it?')
- minimising the person's feelings ('Oh, I wouldn't worry about that.')
- relating it to your own experiences ('Yes, I went there last year – you'll never guess what happened to me …')
- offering advice or easy solutions ('You ought to …', 'What I'd do is …').

Cover the list before the As return to the room and talk for their one minute about their chosen subject, while the Bs do as they have agreed.

Take feedback on how it felt to be in the A group, and reveal the list on the flip chart. Together list on the right-hand side of the sheet what 'good' or 'active' listeners might do. This might include, as well as the 'opposites' of the behaviours previously listed:

- ensuring that the speaker has said everything they want to say
- asking 'open' questions (that encourage exploration and further detail, rather than factual, single word answers)
- 'natural' eye contact and relaxed, open body language
- not sitting directly opposite
- making encouraging noises that say 'I'm listening'
- checking that they have understood ('So am I right in thinking you are saying…?' 'Do you mean…?')
- summarizing/paraphrasing (stopping to sum up every so often : 'So far you've said …')
- showing warmth and empathy and being accepting and genuine.

Next, ask participants to get into groups of three, divided into As, Bs and Cs. This time the As are the listeners, and the Bs the listened to. The Cs are observers and their role is to feedback specifically on any of the skills used by the listeners (using a positive focus).

The Bs begin talking for two or three minutes, and the As model 'active listening skills'.

ACTIVITY 1.3: *Continued*

The Cs then give positive feedback to the listener — concrete and specific examples of what a listener did or said.

The Bs in turn give feedback about what they felt and what qualities and skills they felt a listener had demonstrated.

Finally, the As repeat the positives that they heard from their respective Cs and Bs.

N.B. Although there will not be time in this session for the roles to be rotated, ensure that over the course of the training programme each member has one or more opportunities to try out each role.

Intersessional focus: Applying the learning

Prior to the next session, staff could be asked to use or try out something they have learnt in this session — either in terms of making an environmental change to the classroom, or to the way they relate to pupils, or by using active listening skills in the classroom or staffroom. Staff should be given an opportunity to feed back on the intersessional focus in the way agreed.

Resource Sheet 1: Maslow's hierarchy of needs

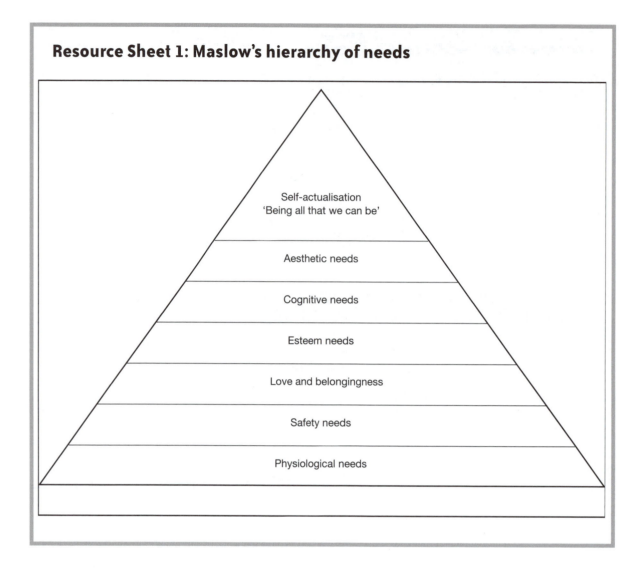

Resource Sheet 2: A model of self-esteem

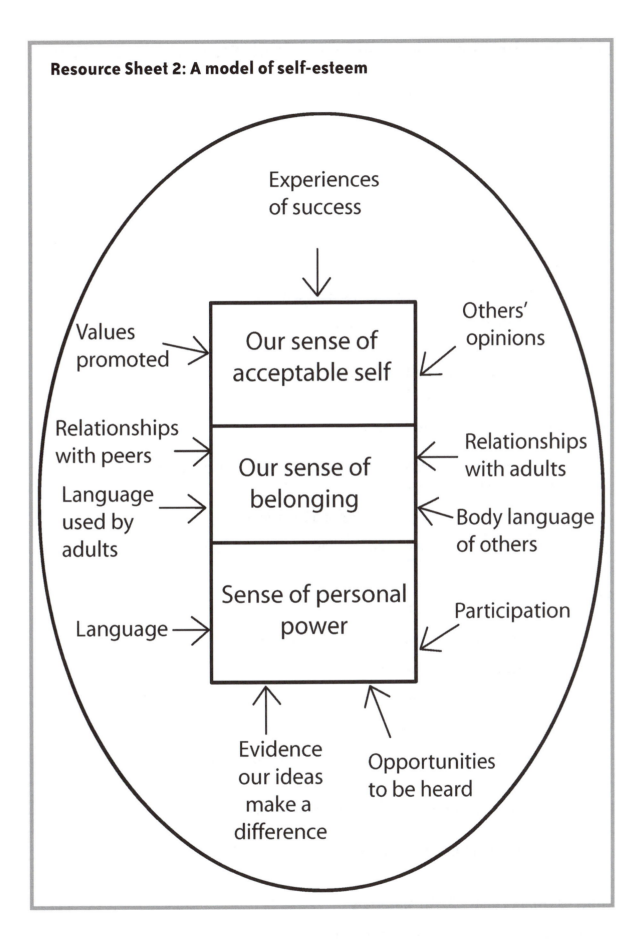

Module 2: Understanding ourselves: feelings, thoughts, behaviour

Suggested timing of session: June/July Year 1

Aims and learning intentions

Staff will

- understand what is meant by self-awareness

- be familiar with the key developmental milestones in self-awareness and the effects of cultural and environmental variation

- be able to explain how feelings, thoughts and behaviour are linked

- apply this understanding to their own contexts and those of the pupils they work with

- be able to explain the role of emotions in learning.

Underpinning concepts and theory

- the development of SEBS pt. 1 – self-awareness: culture, context and key developmental milestones

- the links between thoughts, feelings and behaviour

- the links between emotion and learning.

Resources

- Resource Sheet 3: Pre-session task – Basic Neuroscience

- Resource Sheet 4: Self-awareness as the cornerstone of emotional literacy

- Resource Sheet 5: Self-awareness – My profile

- Resource Sheet 6: The links between feelings, thoughts and behaviour

- Resource Sheet 7: Key factors in teaching about emotions

Useful additional resources for further exploration

- Goleman, D. (1995) *Emotional Intelligence*. London: Bloomsbury.

Links to DfES primary SEAL materials

The development of self-awareness, and in particular the ability to recognize, label and talk about feelings, is a key outcome within all themes of the material. Themes 5 and 6 focus specifically on helping pupils to understand and manage their feelings.

Useful additional resources

■ *Supporting SEAL: Social and Emotional Aspects of Learning.* A set of assembly stories, stimulus stories and whole-school resources to promote a whole-school ethos for developing emotional literacy (Futurelink Publishing, 2005).

Pre-session task

Give each participant a copy of *Resource Sheet 3:* Pre-Session Task, and ask them to read it prior to the Module 2 session, noting down any issues they would like to raise. Explain that there will be time during the session to ask questions, clarify understanding and make links to their teaching practice.

Suggested activities – facilitator's notes

The development of self-awareness

ACTIVITY 2.1	5 minutes

Explain that there are generally considered to be five domains in emotional literacy: self awareness, the management of feelings, motivation, empathy and social skills (including communication). Ask participants to share their understanding of what is meant by self-awareness. Give out Resource Sheet 4: Self-awareness as the cornerstone of emotional literacy and talk through the definition and the following key points.

Key points
■ the arrows demonstrate how self-awareness underlies the development of empathy, managing feelings and social skills

■ emotional and social development is the product of:

a) individual disposition (we have inbuilt differences in our ability to tolerate stress, delay gratification and so on)

b) life experiences, environment and culture (for example, boys are less encouraged to be aware of their feelings in our society)

■ these two elements interact to determine the development of SEBS

■ although there are some important general developmental milestones in self-awareness, the interaction of the 'dispositional' and the 'contextual' factors makes it problematic to chart a general developmental course that could, for example, plot an individual against some norm of development in this area.

Give out Resource Sheet 5: Self-awareness — My profile, and ask participants to complete it if they feel comfortable to do so. Use the guidelines from Chapter 2 on administering a profile. Participants should transfer their score on to Resource 10 from Chapter 2 (see p. 26), as the first part of the profile they will build up throughout the sessions.

Use the following information to explain the scales and offer some ideas for changing and development.

EMOTIONAL SELF-AWARENESS

Definition: Emotional Self-awareness is the degree to which you are able to notice, name and understand your feelings. Emotions are feelings or gut-level instincts or reactions. Unlike thoughts they are not cognitive, but are sensed or experienced and become valuable sources of information about yourself, others and the events and situations around you.

Changing and developing

Check in with your body regularly during the day. Are you uncomfortable, hungry, thirsty, tense?

Make sure you take a second to recognize why you feel the way you do.

Learn a new descriptive word for your feelings every day.

SELF-CARE

Definition: Self-care involves regular habits in the taking care of your body, including nutrition, exercise, rest and hygiene. It means that you practise positive habits — taking the time to give yourself all you need for good health.

Changing and developing

Find an activity that is really good fun for you — like walking, learning salsa, doing circuits, playing netball.

Commit yourself to gradually improving your eating habits.

Don't worry about the 'less good' things you eat! Just keep on eating loads of 'good' things and your poorer choices will gradually lessen naturally.

Explain the following facts about the development of self-awareness (expressing, recognizing and understanding feelings):

■ Some expressions seem to be universal (Ekman, 1992). Ask participants to name what they think the six 'universal' expressions might be (the answers here are: anger, sadness, happiness, surprise, fear, disgust).

■ Children's feelings in response to different situations change in relation to their developmental level, for example, at 5–6-years-old surprise tends to be understood in relation to ignorance ('I didn't know you were coming to pick me up'), while from about 9-years-old onwards it relates more to 'violated expectations' (proving the basis for much humour).

ACTIVITY 2.2 *Continued*

Environmental and cultural influences

It is particularly important to flag up these key points. When we do not recognize or we misread emotional expressions, social interactions are impaired.

Key points

■ Emotional expression varies across cultures. For example, in Izard's (1971) research different groups were asked to identify a range of emotions in Caucasian faces. The results showed that expressions varied portrayed across cultures.

> 83 per cent accuracy for the European sample
>
> 65 per cent accuracy for the Japanese sample
>
> 50 per cent accuracy for the African sample

■ Different emotions are evoked by different situations in different cultures. Many emotions such as pride, shame, guilt and embarrassment depend on sociocultural variables and are therefore felt in relation to different situations in different cultures. These 'social' emotions are explored in Module 9 on pp. 125–132.

■ There are differences in the social conventions regarding the display of emotions. As an example, consider the differences between typical Italian and Japanese greeting rituals.

ACTIVITY 2.3: Application to pupil contexts   **5 minutes**

As a group, ask participants to discuss any cultural variations in conventions or differences in the expression of emotions encountered professionally and/or personally. What are the implications of not teaching about emotions in a multi-cultural society?

Understanding the links between feeling, thoughts and behaviour

ACTIVITY 2.4: Experiencing the links   **15 minutes**

Explain to participants that you are now going to test their individual knowledge of the previous section. (This is a ruse to provoke staff into experiencing the link between feelings, thoughts, and behaviour. This can be introduced in an alternative way, if this is judged to be a high-risk approach for any reason.)

After a few seconds, explain that this is not going to happen, but that you wanted them to have an experience that will shed light on the links between thoughts, feelings and behaviour.

Give out Resource Sheet 6: The links between feelings, thoughts and behaviour, and talk through the components, using the key points below (organized as a 'script'). It will be useful to have a prepared flipchart with three columns – feelings, thoughts and behaviours.

Key points

■ Our behaviour is interlinked with our thoughts and our feelings. Often these are connected to our previous experiences which give 'colour' to the way we will perceive any given situation. This can be thought of as a 'lens' through which we look at the situation.

ACTIVITY 2.4   *Continued*

- Ask participants what 'colour' their lens was when they were told that they were going to be given a test, and what previous experiences might have coloured their lens (perception) in this way.

- This lens will give rise to automatic feelings almost instantaneously. Ask participants what feelings they experienced, and record these on the flipchart.

- These feelings will be accompanied by a range of thoughts (self-talk). Ask participants what thoughts went through their minds, and record these too. The feelings and thoughts interact, with thoughts such as 'I've never been any good at being put on the spot', 'I won't be able to remember anything; I never can', fanning the flames of any feelings of fear or apprehension. Similarly, thoughts such as 'That's not fair' will increase any feeling of anger experienced and so on. Finally, ask participants what they felt like doing. Ask them if they can link this to the thoughts and feelings that they experienced. Some may have become quite overwhelmed by their emotions – feeling disorientated and unable to think clearly, wanting to leave the room, or wanting to respond aggressively. Explain that these responses are quite normal and will be considered in future sessions. Complete the explanation by pointing out the 'feedback arrow' – all experiences influence future perceptions.

ACTIVITY 2.5: Application to pupil contexts   **10 minutes**

Ask participants to talk in pairs about how what they have found out might apply to pupils in their class-rooms, or help to explain some behaviours that they have found puzzling. Take some brief feedback.

The links between emotions and learning
ACTIVITY 2.6: Our beliefs about emotions and learning   **10 minutes**

Place two signs, one labelled 'agree' and one 'disagree' at either end of an imaginary line on the floor. Read out the following statements and ask participants to stand at a position that indicates their degree of agreement. Ask participants to go with their gut feelings and not to worry if they seem to be contra-dicting themselves.

- emotions lead to 'sloppy thinking'
- you must 'rule your feelings, or your feelings will rule you' (Descartes)
- emotions are in fact central to rationality – people need them to think clearly, prioritize and plan (Mayer and Salovey, 1997).

Key points
- Explain that, to a certain extent, those who stood at either end of the continuum are correct. On occasions, emotions certainly can overwhelm our ability to think clearly, but recent research (Ledoux, 1992) suggests that this is true only in extreme situations (during an 'emotional hijack'). For the vast majority of everyday situations and cognitive tasks it seems that the emotions play a crucial role in our motivation and ability to

ACTIVITY 2.6 *Continued*

— direct and sustain our attention

— 'gatekeep' access to our higher thinking skills

— determine what we remember and the extent to which we apply learning.

■ Refer participants to Resource Sheet 3: Pre-session task which they were asked to read beforehand and talk through the key elements of the reading. Explain that these new discoveries have been possible only recently since brain imaging technology has become available, but they are central to understanding the role of the emotions in motivation, learning and behaviour. Allow time for participants to ask questions and clarify their understanding.

Intersessional focus: Helping pupils develop the skills of self-awareness

All children and young people need to become self-aware, in particular in recognizing and being able to label their emotions. We need to support them in developing the skills to do this, both through the environment we create and the explicit teaching we do. Give out Resource Sheet 7: Key factors in teaching about emotions. Before the next development opportunity, reflect upon your actions to support pupils in recognizing and labelling their feelings. Note down everything you do over the course of the day, both formally and informally, to support the development of pupils' skills in this area. Use the resource sheet to consider how your teaching in this area could be improved. If you are using the SEAL curriculum materials, consider how you could further develop the ideas contained within it to increase pupils' self-awareness.

Staff should be given an opportunity to feed back on the intersessional focus in the way agreed.

Resource Sheet 3: Pre-session task – basic neuroscience

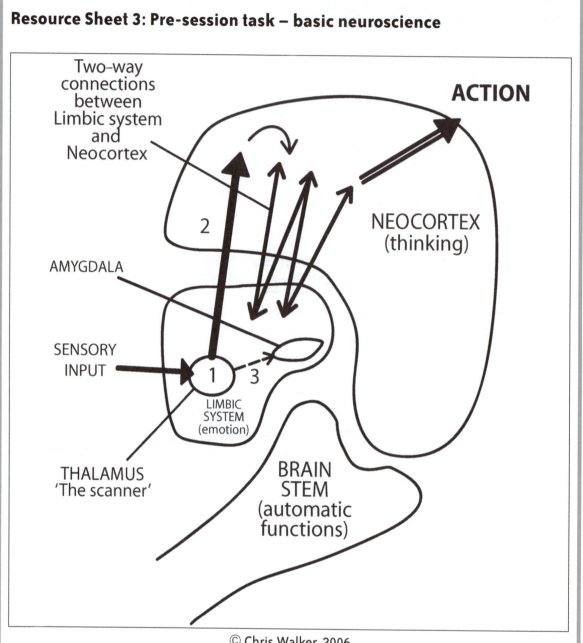

Two-way connections between Limbic system and Neocortex

ACTION

2

NEOCORTEX (thinking)

AMYGDALA

SENSORY INPUT

1   3

LIMBIC SYSTEM (emotion)

THALAMUS 'The scanner'

BRAIN STEM (automatic functions)

© Chris Walker, 2006

We each have three, linked, brain systems: the brain stem – the oldest 'reptilian' part of the brain, which regulates body functions such as breathing and heart-rate; the limbic system (which deals with emotions and life preservaion); and finally, the more recently developed (in evolutionary terms) neocortex which deals with higher mental functions and is associated with 'rationality'.

Traditionally the 'emotional' and 'thinking' systems have been seen as separate, within Western cultures at least, and the rational being valued above the emotional. Brain imaging techniques have, however, allowed us to watch the connections when subjects are engaged in a variety of traditional 'cognitive' tasks – for example, prioritizing, classifying, solving a problem and so on.

This has shown that in order to carry out these tasks, input from the emotional centres (the limbic system) is essential. There are two-way connections between the two systems (shown on the diagram).

The emotional centre carries out several key functions which relate fundamentally to our role as educators.

Gatekeeping function

The thalamus (the entry point for all incoming sensory information) receives a sensory input. The thalamus decides what happens to this sensory information. There are three broad possibilities.

First possibility
If the information is perceived as irrelevant, not linked to any prior knowledge or experience or emotionally of no significance, it will not be processed further (hence children's ability to 'filter' much of what adults talk about) (1).

Second possibility
If it is judged to have significance the information will be sent on from the thalamus to the neo-cortex for processing (2). This takes a little while. At the same time, however, a signal is also sent to a part of the emotional brain called the 'amygdala' (3) — the brain's 'sentry post', which scans all incoming information from the thalamus for potential threats and danger. This signal travels much more quickly and arrives at the amygdala well before the main signal arrives at the neo-cortex.

If no danger is perceived the amygdala takes no further action, and the neo-cortex begins to process the information.

Third possibility
If danger is perceived by the amygdala an 'emotional hijack' will happen (this is explored later in the modules).

The first role of the emotional centre, or limbic system, is therefore that of 'gatekeeper' — it decides what happens to sensory information, whether visual, auditory, kinaesthetic or smell or taste based.

The implication for education is therefore to ensure that what we do and how we do it pass the 'gate-keeper's test' and is perceived as relevant and emotionally stimulating.

Emotional information used in thinking processes

If the information is perceived as of value and relevant, the information will go on to be processed in a number of different ways by the thinking centres of the brain (within the neocortex). It used to be thought that this was the end of involvement for the emotional system.

Recent research however (Ledoux, 1992) shows that this 'rational' processing in fact uses the two way connections between the limbic system and the neocortex, and that far from being the 'enemy' of rationality, emotions are in fact central — without the value tag that emotions attach to different courses of action or outcomes, we would not have any grounds on which to decide between alternatives. Without emotions there would be no motivation to choose one course of action over another, nor would we be able to think clearly, prioritise or plan (Mayer and Salovey, 1997).

The impact of emotional literacy therefore, is that far from causing us to be at the mercy of our emotions; we can use our thinking powers to reflect on them, shape them and moderate them.

The development of emotional literacy thus helps us improve our motivation and our thinking skills, and our thinking helps us to become more emotionally literate.

Resource Sheet 4: Self-awareness as the cornerstone of emotional literacy

Definition

Self-awareness is the ability to recognize and label an increasingly complex range of feelings, and to link these with possible causes. It enables us to have an understanding of ourselves, which becomes our self-knowledge: for example, we come to know our strengths and limitations, how we learn best, what motivates us, and our habitual patterns of feelings and behaviour. We use this knowledge and awareness to anticipate how we might respond and feel in different situations and to modify our behaviour and learning accordingly. Valuing ourselves as individuals is linked to having an accurate awareness of self.

Of Goleman's five domains of emotional intelligence, self-awareness is the one that the others depend on, as shown in the box below by following the direction of the arrows and seeing the domains that each influences most.

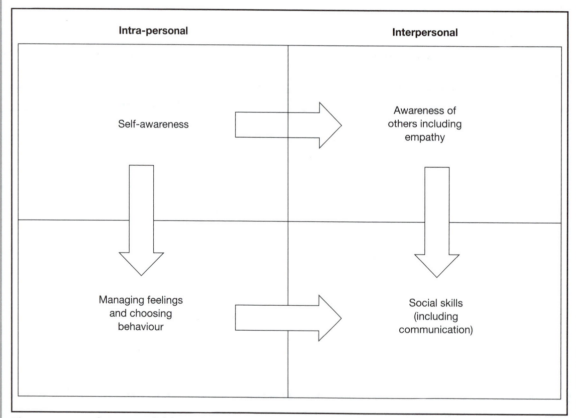

Figure 3.1: Evolving model based on adaptations of others (Morris and Sparrow, 2000; Goleman, 2000; DfES, 2004).

Resource Sheet 5: Self awareness – my profile

To what extent are the following true of you?

Very True – this is how I feel/think/act   **Quite True** – this is quite often true of me and would be recognizable to other people
Seldom True – I don't often think/feel/act like this   **Never true/not true** – I don't think/feel/act like this

Emotional self-awareness questions	Very True	Quite True	Seldom True	Never True
I can name my feelings	3	2	1	0
I have learned a lot about myself by listening to my feelings	3	2	1	0
I am aware of my feelings most of the time	3	2	1	0
I can tell when I am getting upset	3	2	1	0
When I am sad, I know the reason(s)	3	2	1	0
People who show strong emotions scare me	0	1	2	3
I pay attention to my physical state to understand my feelings	3	2	1	0
TOTAL				
GRAND TOTAL				

Score ranges: ◁ 20–21 ◁ 16–19 ◁ 12–15 ◁ 8–11 ◁ 4–7 ◁ 0–3

Self-care questions	Very True	Quite True	Seldom True	Never True
I eat regularly	3	2	1	0
I keep to a desirable weight	3	2	1	0
I avoid excessive sugar, fat, salt	3	2	1	0
I exercise regularly	3	2	1	0
I enjoy or appreciate my body	3	2	1	0
I am aware of tension in my body when it occurs	3	2	1	0
I routinely relax and take time off	3	2	1	0
I avoid smoking and excessive alcohol	3	2	1	0
TOTAL				
GRAND TOTAL				

Score ranges: ◁ 20–24 ◁ 16–19 ◁ 12–15 ◁ 8–11 ◁ 4–7 ◁ 0–3

This page can be photocopied. © *Developing Emotionally Literate Staff*, Morris and Casey, 2006

Resource Sheet 6: The links between thoughts, feelings and behaviour

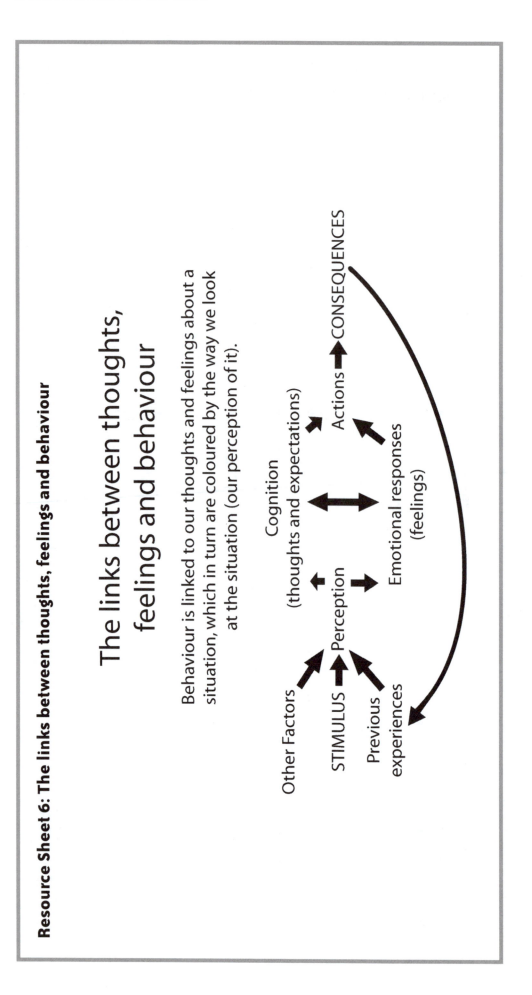

The links between thoughts, feelings and behaviour

Behaviour is linked to our thoughts and feelings about a situation, which in turn are coloured by the way we look at the situation (our perception of it).

Other Factors

STIMULUS → Perception

Previous experiences

Cognition (thoughts and expectations)

Emotional responses (feelings)

Actions → CONSEQUENCES

Resource Sheet 7: Key factors in teaching about emotions

(Adapted from the PNS SEAL Curriculum materials, DfES, 2005)

- Learning opportunities of all types will be most effective within a safe and supportive environment, characterized by trust and openness
- Use a variety of presentation styles to engage learners with auditory, visual and kinaesthetic learning styles, and a variety of stimulus material in different media
- Provide experiential opportunities — we can't learn about emotions without feeling them ...
- Ensure that content is relevant, will link to what learners know, and excites or engages the heart as well as the head (story, poetry, art, music and dance are particularly useful in engaging the emotions)
- Try to make certain that activities are participative and interactive — learners need opportunities to link the learning to what they know and to shape new learning so that it makes sense to them.
- Make sure activities allow learners with different skills, talents, learning styles and intelligences to shine
- Employ a 'working with' approach — learning in this area is life-long
- Take care to provide opportunities for learners to express their own understandings and use active listening techniques — don't impose a view or give the message that there is a single 'right answer'
- Structure sessions to provide 'warm-ups' where possible, a chance to share learning intentions, opportunities for fun and challenge, use different groupings and have a plenary for reflection and sharing learning
- Generalize the learning — use 'teachable moments' to reinforce and consolidate the learning and celebrate and praise attempts to put the learning into practice
- Never tell the learner what they are feeling. When discussing a stimulus (such as a photo or a story) for introducing or building up knowledge about emotions the following questions, adapted from the Guidance to the SEAL resource (DfES, 2005), are useful for ensuring that the 'adult' view is not imposed.

Questions
- What do you think is happening?
- Have you ever been in a situation like this?
- What do you think this person is feeling like?

Encourage the children to say as many words as they can. Add the focus word and other relevant words.

- Have you ever felt like that?
- When have you felt like that?

(This is an opportunity to reinforce the idea that not everyone will have the same feelings in the same situations)

- If you feel like that what would your:
  – face look like?

(encourage them to show you either by modelling or by drawing)

  – body look like?
- If you are feeling like this what might you do?
- If you are feeling like this how does your body feel on the inside?
- Can you think of any other words that might describe the feeling?
- What do you think a person who felt like that would do?

Module 3: Helping pupils to understand and manage their feelings

Suggested timing of session: September Year 1

Aims and learning intentions

Staff will

- know the key skills involved in the management of feelings

- be familiar with the key developmental milestones in managing feelings

- understand the process of an 'emotional hijack'

- have explored some ways to support pupils in resisting impulses by delaying responses.

Underpinning concepts and theory

- the development of SEBS pt. 2 – managing feelings

- the importance of impulse control and delayed gratification

- analysis of an 'emotional hijack' – four key causes.

Resources

- Resource Sheet 8: Pre-Session task

- Resource Sheet 9: The development of our ability to manage our feelings

- Resource Sheet 10: Analysis of an emotional hijack

- Resource Sheet 11: Self-management – My profile.

Useful additional resources

- BBC Video/DVD (2005) Social, emotional and behavioural skills (Programme 1: Dealing with anger).

- *Supporting SEAL: Social and Emotional Aspects of Learning.* A set of assembly stories, stimulus stories and whole-school resources to promote a whole-school ethos for developing emotional literacy (Futurelink Publishing, 2005).

Links to DfES primary SEAL materials

The 'whole-school' problem-solving strategy 'Ready, steady, go, replay' is designed to support pupils in managing their feelings. The 'replay' step encourages the reflection that supports pupils in developing impulse control. Theme 1 offers all pupils an opportunity to develop and share calming down strategies.

Pre-session task

Give out *Resource Sheet 8: Pre-Module task*. Participants are asked to write down what they think is meant by the ability to 'manage our feelings', and to read the information in the resource sheet noting down any queries, examples and issues that arise from the writing. They can then raise these during the session.

Suggested activities – facilitator's notes

Managing our feelings: What is involved?   5 minutes

Remind participants of

- the five domains of SEBS

- the ability to recognize and identify our feelings as a prerequisite to managing them.

Ask participants to refer to the pre-reading for *Resource Sheet 8* and talk through any points that they would like to raise.

The development of the ability to manage feelings   5 minutes

Remind participants of the components of emotional and social development (introduced in Module 2).

- *Individual disposition.* One crucial dispositional difference between individuals is where they sit on the continuum of reflectivity *v.* impulsivity. This continuum reflects the degree to which we mentally evaluate responses before taking action on them. Experiments have shown that even at 4-years-old pupils differ in their ability to resist impulses, and that these differences can persist throughout life (Shoda et al., 1990).

- *Life experiences, environment and culture.* Participants could be asked to consider the differences between how boys and girls are encouraged to deal with their feelings. Different cultures also have strong conventions on the extent to which it is appropriate to display emotions and they differ in the degree to which various emotions are encouraged or discouraged. For example, while Western individualistic societies tend to encourage us to feel and express pride in our achievements, in some cultures pride is seen as deeply undesirable and individuals are encouraged to attribute achievements to external factors, such as luck, or the work of others (Fry and Ghosh, 1980).

ACTIVITY 3.1: Developing skills   10 minutes

Give out Resource Sheet 9: The development of our ability to manage our feelings. In pairs, ask participants to consider the strategies outlined and place them in the order in which they might emerge developmentally. What other strategies can participants identify that are used by children, young people and adults — at what sort of ages do these tend to emerge?

Remind participants that these represent general developmental patterns and are not predictive of the development of a particular individual. The general order of emergence is as follows:

g) (0–3 months); b) (by 1 year); h) (by 1 year) for example, a baby crying when left with a stranger represents an action he or she is taking to try to change a situation; d) and e) (1–3 years); f) (3–5 years); c) (4–5 years) for example tolerating a 'boring' adult conversation by thinking about something exciting, rather than running away or crying loudly; i) (5–7 years). This development is linked to the cognitive shifts that pupils undergo at this time.

Key points:
■ Developmentally, up until the age of about four-years-old, children tend to focus on changing the external situation that is giving rise to uncomfortable feelings.

■ Between four-years-old and seven-years-old they begin to change their strategy — they start to learn to adjust to a situation by changing their internal states. The two mechanisms continue to be used in different situations, with changing the external situation the dominant strategy until the age of 8-years-old, and changing the internal state the preferred strategy by the age of 12-years-old. This ability becomes more sophisticated over time, with children learning a range of strategies to calm down, reframe situations, use positive self-talk, to consider long-term and short-term consequences and so on.

■ In the common strategies used to help children to manage anger (stop–think–do; traffic lights), children must first change the internal state (calming down) then focus on what can be done about situations 'out there'.

Emotional hijacks
ACTIVITY 3.2: What happens during an emotional hijack?   20 minutes

Ask participants to think of a time when they have experienced an extreme of emotion — maybe a time when they felt fury and 'lost it' or behaved irrationally. Ask them to focus on

■ what triggered this response

■ how the feeling built up

■ how it felt at the height of the experience

■ any behaviours that seem, with hindsight, irrational

■ their responses to others during the experience.

ACTIVITY 3.2 *Continued*

If comfortable to do so, they could talk about this in pairs (without having to talk about the context). Take some brief feedback as you go on to Resource Sheet 10 which should be given out at this time. Module 2 focused on the links between the emotional and rational centres of the brain. In some circumstances the two centres become 'disconnected' and the emotional part launches a takeover bid, taking control of the higher rational areas and taking control of the body and our physical responses. This experience has been termed an 'emotional hijack' (Goleman, 1995). An understanding of what it involves, and why it happens, can be extremely useful in understanding pupil behaviour as well as our own. Talk through the following key points below.

Key points

■ The trigger for an emotional hijack is an excess of strong emotion or stress. This might be fear, anger, embarrassment or shock. The example used in the resource sheet is fear. Panic attacks are a form of extreme emotional hijack, while feeling embarrassed and not being able to move or speak with your mind going blank during a presentation and so on, a less severe example.

■ One important difference between individuals is in how much stress or emotion is needed to trigger the hijack. This might be conceptualized as a 'trip-switch' that is set to different degrees of sensitivity in different individuals.

■ The process of an emotional hijack is shown on Resource Sheet 10. The stages are as follows:

1. The 'thalamus' (the entry point for all incoming sensory information) perceives an incoming sensory image (in this case a visual image).

2. Participants will recall from Module 2 that the thalamus sends information to the neocortex but that at the same time sends it (via a quicker route) to the amygdala, the 'sentry' in the brain that scans for danger.

3. If the amygdala detects a certain degree of 'threat' the 'trip-switch' is thrown and the amygdala acts instantaneously, sending messages to the physiological arousal system (via the brain stem) to act. At the same time the amygdala's extensive web of neural connections allows it, during an emotional emergency, to capture and drive much of the rest of the brain – including the rational mind' (Goleman, 1995: 17). For example, the amygdala 'shuffles' memory systems in the brain 'to retrieve any knowledge relevant to the emergency at hand, taking precedence over other strands of thought'. This is what is meant by the term 'emotional hijack' – the emotional brain can be considered to temporarily hijack both the rational brain and our physiology by taking control to keep us alive.

4. The possible responses that this system leads to are 'fight', 'flight', or 'freeze'. Physiological changes begin to instantaneously take place, such as sweating, (so that we don't overheat in the action to follow), increasing heart rate (to get more oxygen to our muscles), the tensing of muscles (ready to run or fight) and so on.

■ This 'fight-or-flight' response is part of our evolutionary history. It is 'hard-wired' and remains important in terms of life-preservation in situations of danger.

■ In less extreme situations, the fight response might manifest itself as verbal aggression or threatening body language, while the flight response is emotional withdrawal.

■ Some children with emotional and behavioural difficulties seem to have 'trip-switches' set to very low thresholds, so that many neutral situations appear threatening to them.

ACTIVITY 3.2 *Continued*

■ Threats are not just physical – they can include threats to our self-esteem or 'street cred', threats to our family name or other cultural or religious beliefs we hold dear.

The causes of emotional hijacks   **10 minutes**
The three main causes of emotional hijack are:

■ The mistake. Because information travels more quickly to the emotional centre than the rational centre (from the thalamus – the brain's 'scanner'), the emotional centre has often responded before we are able to consider the 'whole picture'. The trade-off for speed of response is inaccuracy. Once an emotional hijack is activated, and the rational mind 'captured' by the amgydala, we have often acted before we have had time to think rationally about the situation.

■ The cumulative effect. Sometimes it seems as if people 'explode' for very little reason. Often in these cases, a build up of emotional arousal is the cause. A number of minor irritations that are insignificant on their own can build up stress to the level where it only takes a minor incident to hit the 'trip-switch', resulting in what appears to be a complete over-reaction.

■ Emotional memory. Occasionally, children experience a very strong reaction to a seemingly neutral stimulus or situation. This is because all our memories are stored with an emotional 'tag' within a separate memory system. These emotional memories can persist even when we cannot consciously remember the events that accompanied them. In addition, emotional memories can come to be associated with a sensory input (a smell, a sound or a visual representation) that accompanied the experience, even if unrelated to it. Often we are quite unaware of these emotional associations until they are re-triggered by a seemingly neutral stimulus. It is likely that the child or young person will be unaware of the links and will not be able to explain it, even to him or herself. The behaviours that result from our emotional memories can be the most difficult to understand and respond to.

Theory into practice
■ From this summary, it is clear that in order to support pupils in managing strong feelings, we need to help them find ways to develop strategies to delay any response until the 'thinking' rational part of the brain can 'think straight'. This will usually take just a few seconds, so strategies such as deep breathing, counting to 5, physically relaxing muscles and so on are appropriate.

■ Stress that it is not enough to 'know' a strategy – in order to be useful it must become an automatic response when rising stress is recognized and in order for it to become automatic it will need to be practised over and over again, initially with much scaffolding in place to support it.

ACTIVITY 3.3: Application to adult contexts — 10 minutes

Ask participants to reflect on and share what they do already in helping children to develop these key skills, within the classroom and around the school, both formally and informally.

If a whole-school problem-solving method is used, such as 'stop–think–do' or traffic lights, ask participants to consider how it relates to the learning in this section. (The first steps in most problem-solving models are concerned with delaying response until the rational processes are re-established. Subsequent steps involve the 'thinking' elements such as strategy generation; reframing; considering consequences and so on.)

Intersessional Focus: Helping pupils develop their ability to resist impulses

From the ideas generated, staff can agree on one or two steps to take (either as a group or individually) to improve school practice or consistency in developing pupils' abilities to delay their responses.

Staff can also be given a copy of Resource Sheet 11: Self-management — My profile. As appropriate, offer the following information to staff to support them in interpreting their scores, and remind them to transfer their scores to their score card (see Chapter 2 p. 9).

Self-management leads on from self-awareness and is closely linked to knowing how we can express what we feel in appropriate ways and how we can keep ourselves motivated even on difficult days.

SELF-MANAGEMENT

Definition: Self-expression is one facet of self-management and concerns the degree to which you can express your feelings and gut-level instincts, allowing them to be used as important information as you go about your everyday life. Self-expression saves time, strengthens connections with others and enhances individual and group performance.

Changing and developing

Practice expressing enthusiasm or appreciation.

Make sure you tell people what you are feeling like in everyday conversation.

At least once a day tell someone else how positively you feel about them.

Staff should be given an opportunity to feed back on the intersessional focus in the way agreed.

N.B. Staff should be given an opportunity to feed back on the intersessional focus in the way agreed.

Resource Sheet 8: pre-session task

Write down a few sentences on what you think is meant by the ability to 'manage our feelings'.

Read the information below and note down any queries, examples and issues that arise for you from the writing. You will have a chance to raise these during Module 3.

Managing our feelings

There are two competencies to master in managing feelings successfully. The first involves the ability to promote positive emotional states, for example of calmness and optimism, appropriate to what we are trying to achieve.

Generally, however, the emphasis on managing feelings is placed on the second competency. This involves the ability to modify the immediate impulses triggered by the emotions we experience (for example the urge to hit out when frustrated or angry). To do this we have to be able to:

■ delay our response for a short period in order to allow the 'thinking' part of the brain to get the message (the emotional part responds more quickly)

■ generate alternative strategies that will result in fulfilling our own longer term best interests and those of other people.

The key skills, knowledge and understanding involved in managing feelings are therefore:

■ resisting impulses

■ deferring gratification (knowing that while hitting out might feel good at the time, our best interests are better served by taking a long-term view)

■ having a range of strategies to draw on for dealing with uncomfortable feelings and promoting more facilitative ones.

The aims of supporting pupils in managing their feelings

The view of the authors is that all feelings are important and necessary sources of information, and therefore are not in themselves 'good' or 'bad'. (Although some feel more comfortable than others, uncomfortable feelings serve to spur us to action that will make us feel better.) From this perspective, the aim of managing feelings is not to prevent or suppress feelings of, for example, anger (anger has been the trigger for much positive social change such as civil rights movements), but to enable us to have conscious control and choice over our behaviours in response to these.

Nor is our aim as educationalists to 'extinguish' current ways of dealing with feelings, which might be adaptive and useful mechanisms to 'survive' within certain contexts in which our children operate, but to expand children's repertoires of strategies and to use these in appropriate situations, to enable them to achieve the best long-term outcomes for themselves.

Resource Sheet 9: The development of our ability to manage our feelings

Place the following 'self-management' strategies in the order you would expect them to emerge chronologically. What other strategies would you include at different ages?

a) Using 'internal self-talk' rather than talking out loud to direct one's behaviour

b) Using self-pacifying techniques such as sucking, cooing and babbling

c) Adjusting to a situation that is eliciting uncomfortable feelings by trying to change one's internal state as opposed to trying to change the situation itself

d) Beginning to be able to label emotions, and communicate them to other people

e) Masking a feeling of guilt when lying (that is, demonstrating the ability to differentiate between having a feeling and acting on it)

f) Talking out loud to oneself about one's behaviour in an effort to use self-control

g) Turning one's head away from a stimulus that gives rise to an uncomfortable feeling

h) Taking action to try to change a situation that is giving rise to an uncomfortable feeling, for example moving away from an activity when one of the children's playing becomes aggressive

i) Using logic and reasoning to inhibit impulsive reactions.

Resource Sheet 10: Analysis of an emotional hijack

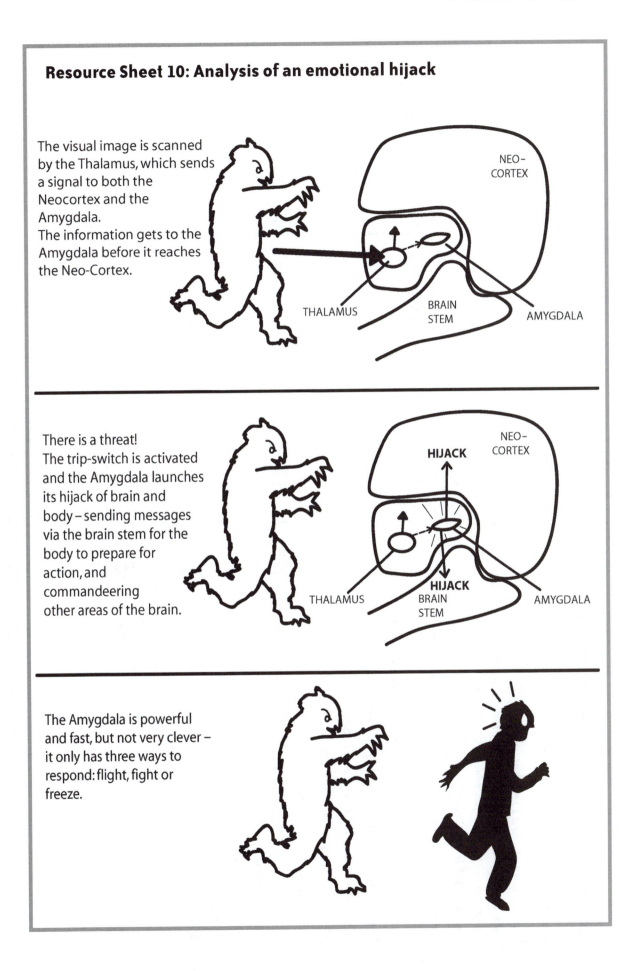

The visual image is scanned by the Thalamus, which sends a signal to both the Neocortex and the Amygdala.
The information gets to the Amygdala before it reaches the Neo-Cortex.

NEO-CORTEX

THALAMUS

BRAIN STEM

AMYGDALA

There is a threat!
The trip-switch is activated and the Amygdala launches its hijack of brain and body – sending messages via the brain stem for the body to prepare for action, and commandeering other areas of the brain.

HIJACK

NEO-CORTEX

THALAMUS

HIJACK

BRAIN STEM

AMYGDALA

The Amygdala is powerful and fast, but not very clever – it only has three ways to respond: flight, fight or freeze.

Resource Sheet 11: Self-management – my profile

To what extent are the following true of you?

Very True – This is how I feel/think/act

Quite True – This is quite often true of me and would be recognizable to other people.

Seldom True – I don't often think/feel/act like this

Never true/not true – I don't think/feel/act like this

Self-management	Very True	Quite True	Seldom True	Never True
I let other people know when I feel pleased about what they are doing. . .	3	2	1	0
I express my emotions even if they are negative	3	2	1	0
I let others know what I want and need	3	2	1	0
My closest friends would say I express my appreciation of them . . .	3	2	1	0
I keep my feelings to myself	0	1	2	3
I let other people know when uncomfortable feelings get in the way of our relationships or roles.	3	2	1	0
I have trouble reaching out to others when I need help	0	1	2	3
I hardly cry, not even at funerals	0	1	2	3
When I'm in a bad mood, I can talk myself out of it	3	2	1	0
I am able to grieve when I lose something important to me	3	2	1	0
TOTAL				
GRAND TOTAL				

△ 25–30
△ 20–24
△ 15–19
△ 10–14
△ 5–9
△ 0–4

Module 4: Dealing with anger and resolving conflict

Suggested timing of session: October Year 1

Aims and learning intentions

Staff will

- be familiar with the process of anger and relate this to their learning on 'emotional hijacks'

- apply their learning to a consideration of school practice

- understand what empathy is, how it develops and variables that can affect its development

- know the key skills and understanding involved in conflict resolution.

Underpinning concepts and theory

- the physiology and process of anger

- the development of SEBS pt. 3 – Empathy

- conflict resolution.

Resources

- Resource Sheet 12: Pre-session task

- Resource Sheet 13: The anger process

- Resource Sheet 14: What is empathy?

- Resource Sheet 15: The development of empathy

- Resource Sheet 16: Empathy – My Profile.

Useful additional resources

- BBC Video/DVD (2005) Social, emotional and behavioural skills (Programme 1: Dealing with anger; Programme 2: Managing Conflict; Programme 4: 2 Tough Crew)

- *Supporting SEAL: Social and Emotional Aspects of Learning.* A set of assembly stories, stimulus stories and whole–school resoures to promote a whole-school ethos for developing emotional literacy (Futurelink Publishing, 2005).

Links to DfES primary SEAL materials

Anger is firstly explored in Theme 2 (Getting on and falling out), and the reasons behind it explored further in Theme 5 (Good to be me). Use of the 'firework' analogy is introduced in Theme 2. Conflict resolution is also tackled in Theme 2.

Pre-session task

Give participants a copy of *Resource Sheet 12: Pre-session task*, which focuses on conflict management. Ask participants to bring their completed sheet to the Module 4 staff session.

Suggested activities – facilitator's notes

Understanding and managing anger

Remind participants about the work covered on managing feelings and 'emotional hijacks' in Module 3. The first part of this module builds on this learning, applying it to the topic of managing anger.

ACTIVITY 4.1: The experience of anger	15 minutes

Ask participants to think of, and note down, a 'trigger' which regularly provokes them to anger. Ask them to focus for a few moments on the situation and on their responses, from the trigger context through to their thoughts and feelings, plus any physiological changes they might experience and their responses to the situation (what they say and do).

Next ask them, after a moment of reflection, to share in pairs any factors that influence their feelings and responses to the situation.

■ Are there times when they don't have an angry response?

■ Are there times when they deal with their feelings in a more, or less, constructive way?

■ What is different about these times?

Take brief feedback for use later in the session.

Give out Resource Sheet 13: The anger process and talk through the following key points.

Key points
■ Several approaches to teaching about anger (including the SEAL materials) use the analogy of the 'firework' to explain the anger process. This has been mapped onto the graph shown on Resource Sheet 13.

■ The trigger becomes the match that lights the fuse of anger. Ask participants to thoughtshower the triggers that they come across with the pupils they teach. Some triggers will be unconscious, as a result of emotional memory (considered in Module 3).

ACTIVITY 4.1: *Continued*

■ The fuse consists of our response to the trigger, physiologically (sweating, heart pounding, muscles tensing and so on) and mentally — the thoughts and feelings we experience in the build-up to the crisis point. Remind participants of the links between thoughts, feelings and behaviour covered in Module 2 — the thoughts we choose to think can intensify or de-escalate feelings, and either accelerate the burning of the fuse or begin to extinguish it.

■ From the learning on emotional hijacks, participants will know that it is of crucial importance for a calming down strategy to be used before a 'takeover' or 'explosion' of anger. Working on recognizing how we feel when we start to get angry is therefore very important — this will be different for everyone. Ask participants for their own first sign that tells them they are becoming angry, and stress the importance of helping pupils to find their own.

■ The explosion is what happens when we 'lose it' or experience an emotional hijack. At this stage we cannot think at all and will not be able to respond rationally to attempts to calm us or influence our behaviour. Remind participants of the work on 'emotional hijacks' in Module 3.

■ The fall-out follows the explosion and consists of our body's attempt to return gradually to a normal level of physiological arousal. This is a key time in which 'flare-ups' are likely given our heightened level of arousal, even up to 45 minutes following the episode. Thoughts and feelings can again play a key part in how extended or rapid this phase is. Sometimes a period of lowness can follow the body's return to normal levels of functioning.

ACTIVITY 4.2: **Application to pupil contexts**   10 minutes

Either:

Ask participants to consider current practice for dealing with behaviours that result from significant anger and also how these fit with the learning about the process of anger. In particular ask them to consider aspects of policy or practice that reflect an understanding of this process and work well, and any policy or practice that might exacerbate difficult situations. What changes might make things better?

Or:

Consider the proactive work that goes on in the school — how does the taught and informal curriculum help pupils to develop strategies to manage their feelings?

ACTIVITY 4.3: **The development of SEBS: Empathy**   10 minutes

Remind participants of the five domains of SEBS and the work covered in Module 2, which stressed the key role of self-awareness and how we need to be aware of our own feelings before we can begin to be aware of the feelings of others.

▶

ACTIVITY 4. 3: *Continued*

Give out Resource Sheet 14: What is empathy? Allow participants a minute or two to read through and comment. Ask them to work in pairs to consider the 'empathic' behaviours listed on the resource sheet and to put them in the chronological order in which they would expect them to occur. Ask participants to share other empathic behaviours they have observed in the age-range worked with, and record these on the flipchart.

Give out Resource Sheet 15: The development of empathy and in pairs ask them to compare this with the judgements they made, and the implications for their age-group of interest. Talk through the following key points.

Key points

- As stressed in previous modules we need to be wary about plotting an individual's 'progress' in this area against a norm as empathy, as with all social, emotional and behavioural domains, is context (and culture) dependent.

- Empathic responses can be encouraged and supported by

  a) using enhancers (relating to similar experiences; identifying similarities) and avoiding diminishers (labelling, stereotyping, prejudices)

  b) Communication skills, for example using active listening (practised in Module 1).

Conflict Resolution

There has been much research in the area of conflict resolution in both adult and child contexts. This section of the module offers an introduction to the area through the lens of children's social and emotional learning, with a focus on empathy.

ACTIVITY 4.4: The tools of conflict resolution   **10 minutes**

Refer participants to the activity they completed as Resource Sheet 12: Pre-session task on conflict management. Record feedback on the factors that hindered or moved things forward towards a resolution from their experiences.

On the flipchart, put up the five key domains of emotional literacy. Ask participants to name any skills, knowledge and understanding they listed as individually necessary for a perfect conflict resolution scenario. Ensure that the following key ingredients are included:

- calming down before tackling the issue

- knowing what outcome you want to achieve and considering whether it is fair to you and the other person

- listening respectfully (without interruptions) so that the other person feels heard

- trying to see the situation from the other person's point of view and acknowledging the importance of this to the other person

- taking turns to have your say

ACTIVITY 4.4: *Continued*   **15 minutes**

■ communicating assertively rather than passively or aggressively

■ generating and exploring a range of solutions

■ agreeing on a 'win—win' outcome, even if this means compromise

■ sticking to what you have agreed.

Intersessional Focus: Application to pupil and adult contexts

Ask participants to consider the learning about conflict resolution for the organization. Request that they specifically consider and note down for sharing (in the agreed forum)

■ What happens already at a whole-school level (for example, the use of peer mediators)?

■ How do I personally help pupils to develop, practise and consolidate the skills of conflict resolution?

■ What could we do better?

Give participants Resource Sheet 16: Empathy — My profile to complete as part of their overall emotional literacy and resilience profile (using the score card and interpretation bands from Chapter 2).

Resource Sheet 12: Pre-session task

Please bring this completed sheet to the Module 4 staff session.

Conflict resolution

Reflect on a recent conflict you have been involved in. This might be from a professional or personal perspective. Focus on and record

- the outcome you were trying to achieve

- the thoughts and feelings you experienced

- your own behaviours — what you said and did

- the other person's behaviour

- which behaviours (both your own and the other person's) hindered the resolution process, and which moved it forward.

List the skills, knowledge and understanding that would be necessary to achieve a perfect conflict resolution scenario, under the following five headings:

Empathy Profile Questionnaire

Self-awareness	
Managing feelings	
Motivation	
Empathy	
Social skills	

Resource Sheet 13: The anger process

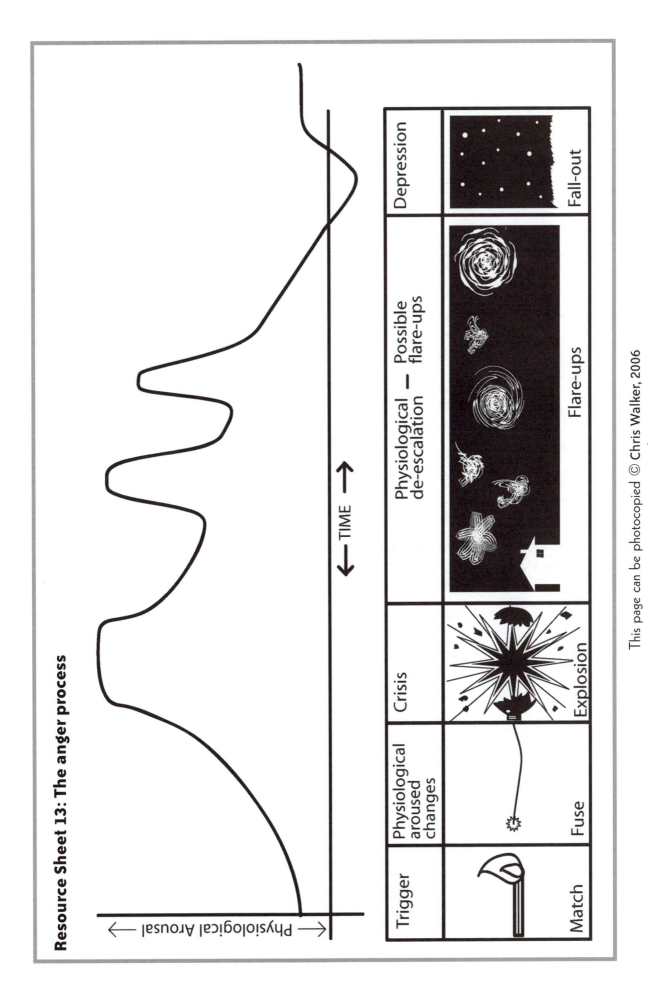

Trigger	Physiological aroused changes	Crisis	Physiological — Possible de-escalation flare-ups	Depression
Match	Fuse	Explosion	Flare-ups	Fall-out

← Physiological Arousal →

← TIME →

This page can be photocopied © Chris Walker, 2006

Resource Sheet 14: What is empathy?

Empathy is the ability to 'tune in' to another person's inner world (feelings, thoughts, motivations and so on) and to see the outside world from that person's perspective. It has three components:

- awareness and knowledge about other people's feelings, thoughts, motivations and so on through 'reading' contextual and other information

- the ability to see things from a different point of view and appreciate the differences in how people feel about things

- the motivation to use an empathic response, in line with another's needs, often subjugating one's own.

Empathy underlies all interpersonal skills, and cannot develop without a basic level of self-awareness (recognizing our own feelings) and understanding (for example, that other people can have feelings just like ours or that people may feel differently from us about the same thing).

Task

In pairs, put the following behaviours in the order in which you would expect them to occur:

- a child gives her own doll to comfort another child who is crying

- a child assumes that other children will dislike playing in the sand because she does

- a child gets as angry with someone who accidentally bumps into him as he does with someone who bumps him on purpose

- a child becomes very concerned about racist activity in the area and starts a school group to counter it.

Resource Sheet 15: The development of empathy

0–1 year

Distress cues from others may elicit own distress responses

1–3 years

Aware of others as distinct from selves

Beginning to understand that others have feelings and thoughts independent of their own, but still adopts an egocentric perspective

3–5 years

Recognizes others' overt expressions of basic emotions

Can work out causes of emotions in 'simple and salient' context

Realises that feelings may change

Able to distinguish intentional from accidental (but weighs consequences over intentions)

6–10 years

Genuine care about feelings of others, protective of friends/family

Can more easily appreciate different point of view

Can infer intentions, feelings, thoughts with accuracy

Recognition of mutual perspective – they may be object of others' perspective

Blame attributed according to intent

Negotiation strategies which meet needs of all involved

9–12 years

Can identify with groups or class of people

Resource Sheet 16: Empathy – my profile

To what extent are the following true of you?

Very True – This is how I feel/think/act

Quite True – this is quite often true of me and would be recognizable to other people

Seldom True – I don't often think/feel/act like this

Never true/not true – I don't think/feel/act like this

Empathy questions	Very True	Quite True	Seldom True	Never True
I can see pain in others even if they don't talk about it.	3	2	1	0
I am able to read people's emotions from their body language	3	2	1	0
I would not hesitate to go out of my way to help someone in trouble. .	3	2	1	0
I take the feelings of others into consideration in my interactions with them	3	2	1	0
I can put myself in someone else's shoes	3	2	1	0
I can forgive myself for not being perfect	0	1	2	3
When I succeed in something, I often think I could have done better. . . .	3	2	1	0
I help others to save face in a tough situation				
TOTAL				
GRAND TOTAL				

BEING AWARE OF OTHER PEOPLE

This section deals with our capacity to be tuned in to and aware of others. It means being empathic and being able to convey this to another person.

EMPATHY AND COMPASSION

Definition: Empathy is the ability to see other people's points of view, recognizing their strengths and limits. Strong performers on this scale are able to accept individual differences and to forgive themselves and others for not being perfect.

Changing and developing

Forgive yourself and others for not being perfect.

Don't let resentment and frustration build.

Get into the habit of talking courageously and respectfully to others.

Practise imagining what other people's lives are like.

Module 5: Working together

Suggested timing of session: November Year 1

Aims and learning intentions

Staff will

- be aware of the effects of the hidden social and emotional demands of classroom tasks set

- be familiar with research findings about the value of group work and guidelines for 'best practice'

- be aware of the range of social, emotional and behavioural skills needed for effective group participation

- know how to structure group work to support the development of pupils' SEBS.

Underpinning concepts and theory

- the social and emotional demands of group work

- skills involved in group work

- principles of effective cooperative group work.

Resources

- Resource Sheet 17: Pre-session task

- Resource Sheet 18: Group observation checklist

- Resource Sheet 19: Principles of effective group working and implications for practice.

Useful additional resources

- BBC Video/DVD (2005) Social, emotional and behavioural skills (Programme 3: Working together).

- DfES (2004) *Pedagogy and Practice: Teaching and learning in secondary schools:* Unit 10 Group Work.

- DfES (2004) *Primary National Strategy – Professional development materials: Classroom community, collaborative and personalised learning.*

- DfES (2003) 'Speaking, Listening, Learning'.

Links to DfES primary SEAL materials

Theme 2 focuses specifically on the skills of cooperation and working as a group. Each of the themes provides opportunities to practise and develop group-working skills.

Pre-session task

Give participants *Resource Sheet 17: Pre-session task* which relates to good practice in group working. Ask them to read this information before coming to the session, and to be ready to consider their own practice in relation to it during the session.

Suggested activities – facilitator's notes

The importance of group working

- Being able to work as part of a group is a critical skill in all contexts – school, life and work. In a survey of what employers look for in entry-level workers (Goleman, 1998: pp. 12–13) 'out of seven desired traits, just one was academic: competence in reading, writing and math'. Five of the others involved applicants' social and emotional skills:

    - listening and oral communication
    - adaptability and creative responses to setbacks and obstacles
    - personal management, confidence, motivation to work toward goals and take pride in accomplishments
    - group and interpersonal effectiveness, cooperation and teamwork, skills at negotiating disagreements
    - effectiveness in the organization, wanting to make a contribution, leadership potential.

- In educational settings, much learning takes place in social situations such as group and pair work and we need to be aware of the social and emotional demands of the tasks we set pupils, particularly when we ask them to work in groups.

ACTIVITY 5.1: The social and emotional aspects of working with others   15 minutes

Ask participants to work with someone that they do not usually work with. Set each pair the task of agreeing and ranking the five most important social and emotional skills that enable effective group work to take place in the classroom. Give them three minutes for this task. Use a flipchart to record feedback.

Explain that while they have focused on the cognitive content or outcome of the task, there are other dimensions involved in working with other people that are of equal importance. Ask participants to consider the process of working with someone they do not tend to work with under two headings: emotional demands and social demands. 'Unpick' this by asking them to record any feelings they experienced and had to 'deal with', and any social skills that they were conscious of using.

Take feedback under each heading. General social demands might include:

- establishing a rapport

- using eye contact and smiling to encourage each other

- using exaggerated listening behaviours

- taking care not to interrupt.

Eliciting emotional responses can be a challenge so be ready to use the examples below of how other groups have often felt in this situation:

- apprehensive

- uncertain about whether they have understood the task correctly

- worried that their answers may be rejected or scorned

- pressurised to 'come up with something' in the time limit.

Skills used might include managing these feelings and appearing confident even when not feeling it.

Key points

- This activity aims to offer some insight into the social and emotional demands of working with others. Ask participants to reflect for a moment on how their own experiences during this activity might be magnified for children in the classroom.

- Research (Linn and Burbules, 1994) shows the importance of paying attention to the social and emotional demands of group work. There is much evidence that cooperative group working is effective in improving attainment compared with children working alone (Johnson and Johnson, 1999) – the talking and thinking involved in group processes help to develop many higher order skills. However, where group interaction is disrespectful or unequal, the use of group work is actually negatively related to achievement. Activity 5.1 can help us to understand the emotional and social costs of 'getting it wrong' for children.

This session aims to support staff in understanding the factors involved in getting group work right, to raise achievement and provide a context for developing children's social skills.

The skills involved in group work
ACTIVITY 5.2: The world's worst group   15 minutes

Ask participants to work in two or three small groups to draw up a poster illustrating or representing the 'world's worst group'. For each group appoint one observer whose role is to complete Resource Sheet 18: Group observation checklist. This person should not interact with the group at all during the task.

Facilitative questions to stimulate ideas could include:

■ What gets on your nerves when working in a group?

■ What would the group look like from the outside?

■ What would be going on? What would people be doing or saying?

■ What would you hear?

■ How would people be feeling?

■ How would you feel if you walked in on the group?

Ask a spokesperson to talk through the main features of their group's poster (two minutes per group). Common problems that might be identified include:

■ one member dominating the group, while others opt out passively or actively, deliberately engaging in off-task behaviours

■ people not listening to each other, not showing respect and using personal put-downs

■ lack of cooperation – for example, no-one wanting to take on the 'boring' roles, lack of cohesiveness, no shared purpose, low motivation, conflicts emerging and not being dealt with

■ failure to consider or get to know the individual strengths and weaknesses of individuals and a lack of clear roles.

Ask participants to list the skills that would turn the 'world's worst group' into the 'world's best group', adding to the list of skills compiled in Activity 5.1. Ask the observers in each group to share their own observations about aspects of the group process that were particularly facilitative. N.B. Take care that the focus stays positive and that individuals are not singled out for negative comment.

If appropriate, offer the following list of 'Skills we can expect of most Y7 pupils', which comes from Pedagogy and Practice: Group Work (2004b):

■ speak in turn

■ listen to others' point of view

■ participate, respond and make suggestions

■ cooperate within a small group

■ take on a given role (for example, recorder or chair)

■ adopt a lead role if requested

■ help make sure that the task is completed

■ engage in exploratory talk.

▶

ACTIVITY 5.2 *Continued*

From the perspective of social and emotional skills we might add:

■ being aware of our own feelings and managing these in ways that do not impact negatively on the group

■ being aware of the feelings of others in the group and responding empathically to these.

Stress that we actively need to teach these skills and reinforce them in and out of the classroom whenever possible. Before pupils can work effectively in groups, they need our support in developing the necessary skills. We can do this by

■ structuring group work supportively

■ explicitly focusing on the 'process' aspects of group working.

ACTIVITY 5.3:   What do we do to foster the development of these skills?   10 minutes

Draw a rating scale (0–10) on the flipchart with one end (0) labelled 'No support' and the other (10) as 'Coherent and effective policy and practice in developing group work skills'. Ask participants to rate individually where they feel the school as a whole would sit on this scale in terms of supporting children in developing group-working skills.

Ask participants to work in year or key-stage groups as appropriate to consider

■ why they have chosen their particular rating (e.g. what they do in the classroom/school that means that the rating is not lower)

■ what would have to happen for them to move their rating towards an 'ideal' (perhaps drawing on their thoughts from Activity 5.2 to help formulate a vision of what this 'ideal' might look like)

Take feedback or ask for notes to be made which can then be collated and circulated as appropriate.

Principles for setting up supportive group-work opportunities
ACTIVITY 5.4:   Application to pupil contexts   **15 minutes**

Refer participants to Resource Sheet 17: Pre-Session task, which raises many issues about the way we organize group working and has implications for our practice.

Give out Resource Sheet 19: Principles of effective group working and implications for practice and ask participants to note down aspects of their current practice that fit well with the 'good practice' findings (drawing on their pre-reading) and any implications for change they could make.

Intersessional focus: Getting group work right

The intersessional focus should be on the use of group working within the classrooms. Practitioners could be asked to make a note of current practice, what tasks groups are asked to complete, how they are structured, what 'process' information they are given and so on. This practice could then be compared against the information they have on good practice and one or more changes identified and implemented. N.B. Staff should be given an opportunity to feed back on the intersessional focus in the way agreed.

Resource Sheet 17: Pre-session task

Please read the following information and be ready to draw upon it in relation to your own practice during the session (Module 5). Please note down any questions, examples and issues that are raised for you by the reading. There will be time during Module 5 to raise these.

Group work: Theory into practice
This reading is summarized from Pedagogy and Practice – Unit 10 Group work (DfES, 2004b).

- Group work: there are two different types of group work we might engage with in the classroom. These are group opportunities
  - specifically for developing group-work skills (for example, circle times that focus on taking turns and setting group tasks that cannot be completed without cooperation)
  - with a subject-related focus which provide opportunities for children to practise their group-working skills (for example by making explicit the 'process' aspects of the group as well as focusing on the content outcomes achieved).

- Structuring the group: there are many different ways of organizing groups in the classroom, each with advantages and disadvantages. Research suggests that for cooperative group work the most effective groups are those that include children of different ability levels (in relation to the content of the task) as long as these are not too different.

  'Groups composed of high and medium, or medium and low achievers gave and received more explanations than students in high-medium-low ability groups. When students of the same ability are grouped together, high-ability students thought it unnecessary to help one another, while low-ability students were less able to do so.' (Webb, 1991; Askew and William, 1995)

- Structuring the session: successful sessions include
  - Opportunities for children to give and receive help. Children may need support in being encouraged to ask questions of each other. Remind participants of the importance of creating a safe environment within which the group will operate. The setting of ground-rules can help to create this safe environment. Children will also need support in giving 'useful' sorts of help, for example being taught that offering 'the correct answer' without explanation doesn't help the questioner.
  - An opportunity for the group to reflect on how well it performed and how to improve. Holding a 'plenary' or debriefing session using a standard structure can work well. The children could be asked to focus on: What went well? What didn't go so well? What could we do differently next time?
  - Individual goals for specific aspects of the task as well as group goals. Having individual goals helps to prevent children 'opting out'. One idea for motivating children is to give both group and individual ratings; another is to ensure that a variety of roles (for example, scribe, time-keeper, leader) are assigned.
  - A sense that the group's success depends on whether they work together or not. This could be encouraged by making the process focus explicit, and specifically valuing and celebrating cooperative behaviours and so on. Using observers can also have this effect.

- Support where necessary in helping children to use the interpersonal skills necessary for group working. Examples of where support might be needed are in sharing (resources and time), in communication and participation, in leadership, in decision making and in conflict resolution.

- Sensitively timed and directed adult support. Adults need to learn to strike a balance between enabling the children to work things out for themselves, and intervening to 'move things on' when the group gets stuck.

■ Structuring the task. Successful sessions show the following characteristics (to consider when structuring group tasks):

- the goals and desired outcomes of the activity are clearly stated

- an explicit focus on 'process' aspects when the task is being explained, making it clear that cooperation is necessary

- roles are assigned so that everyone knows what is expected of them.

Resource Sheet 18: Group observation checklist

	Examples/Evidence
Did everyone feel OK about being in the group?	
How effective was the planning process?	
Did everyone get to have their say?	
Did people listen to others?	
Were clear roles assigned?	
Did people feel safe to ask, question, disagree with others?	
How were differences of opinion resolved?	
Were group members supportive of each other?	

This page can be photocopied. © *Developing Emotionally Literate Staff*, Morris and Casey, 2006

Resource Sheet 19: Principles of effective group working and implications for practice

Focus	Area of Good Practice Findings (refer to Pre-session task for further detail)	What I do now	What I will do differently
Structuring the group	Ability mix		
Structuring the session	Opportunities for peer support		
	Opportunities for reflection on group performance		
	Individual and group goals		
	Success as a group issue		
	Support for interpersonal skills		
	Adult support		
Structuring the task	Goals and desired outcomes		
	Explicit focus on 'process' aspects		
	Assigning roles		

Module 6: Motivation, persistence and resilience

Suggested timing of session: January Year 2

Aims and learning intentions

Staff will

- be aware of a range of internal and environmental factors that affect motivation

- be familiar with intrinsic, external and internal motivation

- understand how motivation, persistence and resilience affect performance in learning

- know a range of strategies for supporting the development of internal motivation, persistence and resilience (including the design and structure of learning tasks)

- have reflected on how this learning relates to teaching and learning.

Underpinning concepts and theory

- the development of SEBS pt. 4 – motivation, persistence and resilience

- internal, external and intrinsic motivation

- locus of control

- the design and structure of learning opportunities to develop internally-motivated learners.

Resources

- Resource Sheet 20: Pre-session task

- Resource Sheet 21: Motivation

- Resource Sheet 22: A model of performance

- Resource Sheet 23: Setting tasks to develop internal motivation

- Resource Sheet 24: Resilience – My profile.

Useful additional resources

- *Classroom community, collaborative and personalised learning* (DfES, 2004)

- *Pedagogy and Practice: Developing Effective Learners* (DfES, 2003)

■ *Supporting SEAL: Social and Emotional Aspects of Learning.* A set of assembly stories, stimulus stories and whole-school resources to promote a whole–school ethos for developing emotional literacy (Futurelink Publishing, 2005).

Links to DfES primary SEAL materials

Theme 4 (Going for Goals!) deals specifically with the attitudes and beliefs that foster motivation, persistence and resilience.

Pre-session task

Give out *Resource Sheet 20: Pre-session task* and ask participants to read it prior to the staff session for Module 6. Ask participants to record any queries, examples or issues that arise for them from the reading. There will be time to explore these during the Module 6 session.

Suggested activities – facilitator's notes

Exploring motivation

ACTIVITY 6.1: External, internal or intrinsic?	10 minutes

Give out Resource Sheet 21: Motivation. Split participants into two groups. Ask Group A to reflect for a minute or two on a situation in which they felt motivated and enthused by a particular goal they wanted to achieve, focusing on the headings (A). They should be prepared to give brief feedback throughout the session on their responses, if they feel comfortable to do so.

Ask Group B to reflect on a situation in which they had to achieve a goal or outcome but did not feel motivated or enthused, completing the 'B' options on the resource sheet.

Refer participants to Resource Sheet 20: Pre-session task, and draw their attention to the section entitled: Types of motivation and developmental patterns. Recap on external, internal and intrinsic motivation.

Ask participants in Groups A and B to share their responses, and in particular to indicate what they believe was the 'prime motivator' in their scenario. Note that these are not always clear-cut categories, and many of our undertakings are influenced by all three.

ACTIVITY 6.2: What inspires and sustains motivation?	5 minutes

Ask one person to act as scribe, while participants, drawing on their responses to the previous activity, in turn complete the sentence: 'To be motivated to accomplish something challenging I need … '

Examples might include: 'to feel that the outcome matters'; 'to do it my way'; 'to break it down into do-able chunks'.

It is important that we use this knowledge to set up situations in which pupils are more likely to feel motivated.

Draw participants' attention to the importance of the concept of 'locus of control' (explained in the reading) and its link to motivation.

ACTIVITY 6.3: Application to pupil contexts   **15 minutes**

Give out Resource Sheet 22: A model of performance and ask participants to reflect on the factors impacting on motivation. Are there any additions or modifications that they would suggest, or points needing clarification?

Ask each pair to consider a task that they have set in the past week for pupils to achieve. How well did the task motivate pupils and what was it about the task that facilitated or hindered the degree of pupils' internal motivation (in relation to the factors included in the model)?

Take brief feedback — what were the general strengths in staff's use of what we know about motivation to engage pupils? What were the areas for development?

Persistence and resilience

Two further key areas contributing to 'performance' are persistence and resilience (refer to Resource Sheet 22). Even when we are motivated initially, it is often hard to keep going (persist) or bounce back after a knock back or disappointment (resilience). The following Activity (6.4) will offer some helpful strategies for both adults and pupils.

Key points

Examples of the strategies listed on the resource sheet include:

- *Reframing*: 'I bunked off three lessons today' versus 'You went to three lessons'.

- *Using positive self-talk*: 'I've overcome problems like this in the past'; 'I can't do this yet, but I will be able to with more practice'.

- *Challenging 'faulty thinking'*

  - black and white thinking: 'I'll never be able to do this'.

  - magnifying the significance: 'If I mess this bit up there's no point in carrying on'.

  - catastrophizing: 'I know I'm not going to get this in on time, then I'll fail my GCSE and won't get a job, my parents will throw me out … '.

  - Global judgements: 'If I can't do this, I must be stupid … '.

- Keeping the big picture in mind: Imagining or writing down the eventual benefits.

- Building in rewards: 'When I've done this little bit, I will buy myself that video'.

ACTIVITY 6.4: 'Keeping on keeping on'   **5 minutes**

To elicit further strategies that aid persistence and resilience, ask participants to take part in a round (scribing responses) completing the sentence: 'When the going gets tough, I … '

Examples might include: I tell myself … ; I visualise the finished project; I think of a role model; I break the task down further; I set a target of spending ten minutes on it and reward myself.

The school context
ACTIVITY 6.5: Helping pupils develop internal motivation
10 minutes

Give out Resource Sheet 23: Setting tasks to develop internal motivation and talk through the key points. So far in the module, they have considered the beliefs, attitudes and environmental conditions that are likely to result in pupils (and adults) being internally motivated to undertake a task or achieve a goal, as well as some strategies for developing persistence and resilience. This section of the module considers how staff might design and structure learning tasks and processes to help develop internal motivation.

Key points
Motivation will be high when teachers plan learning opportunities with regard to

■ Learning style: We all have a favoured style of taking in and processing new information — visual (diagrams, pictures, mind-maps and so on); auditory (lectures, radio broadcasts); kinaesthetic (moving around, role-plays). The key issue for teaching is to ensure information is presented in different sensory modalities, so that learners of all preferences will be motivated.

■ Utilising Multiple Intelligences: This theory (Gardner, 1983) holds that there are many different ways we can be intelligent, not just the 'academic' intelligence traditionally valued in education, but linguistically, mathematically, spatially, musically, kinaesthetically, naturalistically, interpersonally and intrapersonally (the two types of intelligence focused on in emotional literacy). Motivation is enhanced in those schools which value and celebrate the different intelligences displayed by students, and structure learning opportunities to ensure that each is recognized, and that all pupils have an opportunity to shine.

■ Relevance and interest to the individual: Remind participants of what happens to information that the brain registers as of no relevance, or emotionally 'flat' (see Module 2 pp. 52–64).

■ Pitched to challenge: It is important that the task is pitched not so low that the learners' skills exceed the challenge (resulting in boredom), nor so high that it makes impossible demands on skills (resulting in anxiety). Both boredom and anxiety are detrimental to motivation.

■ Opportunities to review performance: This aspect is important to enable pupils to celebrate their successes and to adapt their future efforts. The use of a plenary is beneficial for this purpose.

Intersessional focus

This builds on the module activities. Participants are asked to use the learning from the session to plan an activity that will encourage pupils to be internally motivated.

A further activity is to complete the personal profile in the area of resilience (Resource Sheet 23). An interpretation guide is included, and participants should be reminded of the guidelines from Chapter 2 in completing it (see p. 37), and the need to transfer their scores to the scoring grid (also found in Chapter 2 p. 26).

N.B. Staff should be given an opportunity to feedback on the intersessional focus as agreed.

Resource Sheet 20: Pre-session task

An overview of motivation
Definition

Motivation is what prompts us to engage with experiences, to set ourselves long- and short-term goals, and achieve these through planning, persisting in the face of frustration, boredom or obstacles and being able to bounce back after setbacks and disappointments. It has a significant influence on our ability to direct our attention, concentrate for increasing lengths of time, and to resist distractions.

Types of motivation and developmental patterns.

Motivation can come from outside (the promise of reward or a threat of a negative consequence), that is external motivation; or from within ourselves (overcoming short-term discomfort for the sake of a later longer-term gain), that is internal motivation; or it can come from the activity or experience itself (because it is pleasurable in itself), that is intrinsic motivation.

As babies we start out by being motivated purely by intrinsic pleasure or an aversion to unpleasant stimuli. As we grow older, we learn to modify our behaviour and resist immediate impulses for a promised reward or the threat of a negative consequence, and can delay gratification for increasingly longer periods. Children begin to become internally motivated from about the age of 6-years-old.

However, it must be remembered that we are all motivated to different degrees and in different contexts by all three types of motivation — we eat chocolate because it tastes good; we work on an essay because we want to obtain our degree; we go to work because we get paid (even though we may also enjoy it!).

Skills needed

Both internal and external motivation involve the fundamental skills of impulse control and the ability to delay gratification to achieve a longer-term goal. (These are introduced in Module 3 in relation to managing feelings; see p. 72.)

Also involved are the skills of self-awareness and managing feelings — recognizing our own strengths and limitations, and how we learn best in order to devise and achieve appropriate goals. We need to be able to recognize feelings that we ourselves experience and to put in place strategies for reducing or changing these into more positive states, thus overcoming feelings of frustration when learning something new, or moving on from a disappointment to try a new way of solving the problem (persistence and resilience).

In addition to the skills listed above, our degree of motivation is fundamentally affected by:

- The nature of the task — do we think it is in any sense achievable?

- The beliefs we hold about our ability to achieve the goal.

- Our beliefs about where success (or failure) will come from — our beliefs about this are called our locus of control. This can be internal where we believe that the outcome will be attributable to factors within our control, that we can influence the outcome through, for example, hard work or practice. An external locus of control on the other hand means that we put success or failure down to external factors such as luck, other people, our tools or even the weather.

- The degree of personal responsibility we feel for our goals and actions in achieving the task.

- Whether we adopt an optimistic or a pessimistic attitude.

The importance of environment and context

Our motivation and resilience are heavily dependent on context and the current demands on us. In facilitative contexts where we are encouraged and viewed positively and where failure is seen as a learning opportunity it will feel safe to take a risk and try something new, knowing that if it all goes wrong it won't be the end of the world, and hope will always spring eternal (think of the motivational effects of the National Lottery!).

As we know from Maslow's Hierarchy (see Module 1 Resource Sheet 1) our motivation to learn and engage fully with learning opportunities will not be satisfied if other lower needs are not being met. Resilience will be lowered when we are tired, stressed or coping with strong emotion.

To take risks requires a positive sense of self-esteem as a learner and a person (see Modules 1 and 7).

The role of emotions

Motivation is inextricably linked to our emotions — it is the emotional value that we attach to our actions and goals that get us out of bed in the morning, draws us towards certain activities, people or experiences, and helps us to persist when things are difficult by imagining the 'big picture' and future satisfactions.

Resource Sheet 21: Motivation

Please record briefly

■ The factors that motivated you to undertake the activity or 'go for goal' (A and B)

■ The feelings you experienced when you committed yourself to it (A and B)

■ How you went about planning to achieve your goal (A and B)

■ Any aspects of the environment that supported you (A), or hindered you (B) in achieving the goal

■ Any other specific factors that helped or encouraged you (A) or hindered you (B)

■ What social and emotional skills or strategies you used or needed (A and B) to achieve your goal particularly in relation to any obstacles or disappointments or discouraging thoughts or feelings.

Resource Sheet 22: A model of performance

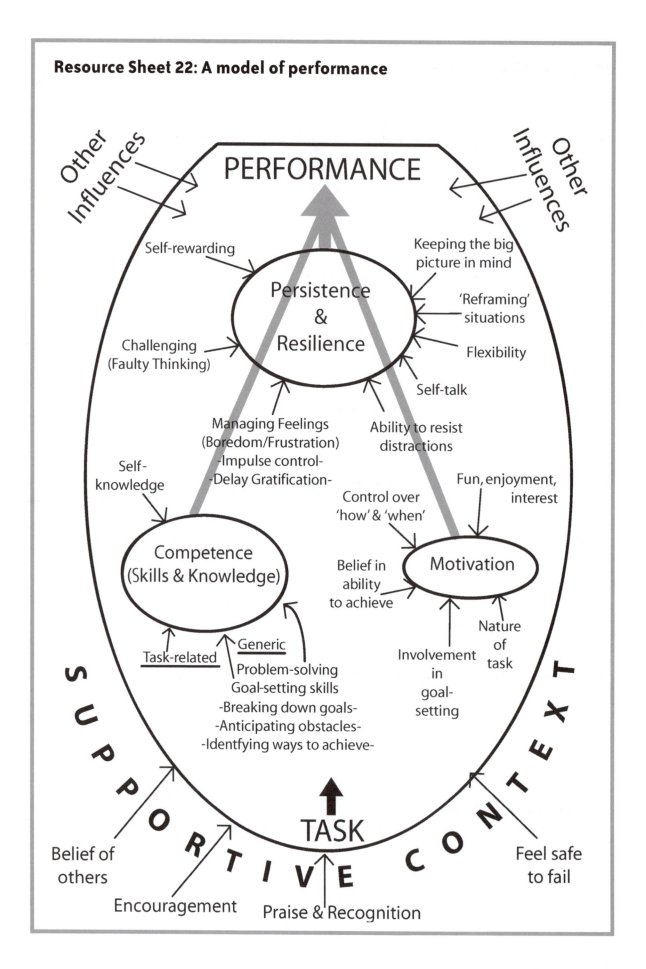

Resource Sheet 23: Setting tasks to develop internal motivation

The nature of the task itself is of key importance in developing motivation skills.

Internally motivated learning will be promoted when tasks are provided within a facilitative environment in which it feels safe to take a risk and this engages learning opportunities which

- match the learning style of individuals
- offer individuals a chance to 'shine' using their particular type of intelligence
- are of relevance and interest to the individual
- build on something they already understand
- offer the opportunity for some control by the learner
- provide an appropriate degree of challenge
- supply opportunities for learners to review their performance, celebrate successes and adapt their future efforts.

Resource Sheet 24: Resilience – My profile

To what extent are the following true of you?

Very True – This is how I feel/think/act
Quite True – This is quite often true of me and would be recognizable to other people.
Seldom True – I don't often think/feel/act like this
Never true/not true – I don't think/feel/act like this

Resilience questions	Very True	Quite True	Seldom True	Never True						
I can bounce back after feeling disappointed	3	2	1	0						
I can accomplish what I need to if I put my mind to it	3	2	1	0						
Obstacles or problems in my life have resulted in unexpected changes for the better	3	2	1	0						
There is always more than one right answer	3	2	1	0						
I know how to satisfy all parts of myself	0	1	2	3						
I am not one to procrastinate	3	2	1	0						
I am afraid to try something again when I have failed at it before	0	1	2	3						
I decide certain problems are not worth worrying about	3	2	1	0						
I relax myself when tension builds up	3	2	1	0						
I can see the humorous side of situations	3	2	1	0						
I often put things aside for a while to get a perspective on them	3	2	1	0						
When something is not working I try to come up with an alternative plan	3	2	1	0						
TOTAL										
GRAND TOTAL										

Score ranges: △ 28–36 △ 24–27 △ 18–23 △ 12–17 △ 6–11 △ 0–5

OUTCOME

RESILIENCE

Definition: Resilience is your ability to bounce back, to be flexible, to retain a sense of curiosity and hopefulness about the future, even in the face of adversity.

Changing and developing

Think of a time when you turned a setback into a triumph. Write it down.

Keep asking yourself how else you might think of a situation.

Take regular breaks, especially after a loss or setback.

Module 7: Supporting pupils' self-esteem

Suggested timing of session: March Year 2

Aims and learning intentions

Staff will

- understand the importance of self-esteem
- develop their understanding of the three components of self-esteem, in particular how the 'our sense of acceptable self' develops and changes
- be familiar with behaviours indicating high or low self-esteem and the cycle by which these can be sustained
- have a range of strategies to develop and sustain pupils' self-awareness and raise their self-esteem through the environment, adult modelling and the provision of learning opportunities.

Underpinning concepts and theory

- models of self-esteem
- locus of control
- 'Multiple Intelligences' and learning styles.

Resources

- Resource Sheet 25: Pre-session task (The importance of self-esteem)
- Resource Sheet 26: The cycle of low self-esteem

Useful additional resources

- *Classroom community, collaborative and personalised learning* (DfES, 2004)
- *Pedagogy and Practice: Learning styles* (DfES, 2003).

Links to DfES primary SEAL materials

The SEAL resource is based on the belief that children's self-esteem will be raised as they learn the skills of emotional literacy. In addition the 'key messages' promoted and learning opportunities offered throughout aim to support children in valuing themselves and others. Theme 5 'Good to be me' relates most specifically to the area of self-esteem.

Pre-session task

Give out *Resource Sheet 25:Pre-Session task,* and ask participants to read it prior to the staff session for Module 7. Ask participants to record any queries, examples or issues that arise for them from the reading. There will be time to explore these during the session.

Suggested activities – facilitator's notes

Understanding self-esteem	5 minutes

Recap on the pre-session activity and offer an opportunity for participants to share their responses.

ACTIVITY 7.1: Self-esteem and behaviour	10 minutes

Ask participants to discuss (in pairs or small groups) behaviours particularly in learning that characterize high and low self-esteem. Take feedback, adding the key points below if necessary.

Key points

■ High self-esteem can be thought of as emotional capital or 'money in the pocket' (Maines and Robinson, 1999) which helps us to be prepared to take risks in trying something new, allows us to accept failure or criticism without 'crumbling' and enables us to hear and believe praise which, in turn, further supports our good self-esteem. High self-esteem is associated with positive expectations and optimistic thinking.

■ Low self-esteem makes us afraid to risk failure by trying something new and defensive in the face of criticism or adverse circumstances, preventing us from accepting praise as we accept only what we already believe. Low self-esteem leads to negative expectations, pessimistic thoughts and feeling down and these become self-fulfilling prophecies, further confirming the scant value that we place on ourselves.

ACTIVITY 7.2: Where do 'self-image' and 'ideal selves' originate?	15 minutes

Ask participants to imagine a long line on the floor in the staffroom. One end of the line represents the 'brilliant' end, the other 'terrible'. Then ask them to position themselves along this line in relation to their ratings of their ability in the following areas:

'completing crosswords', 'learning difficult things', 'driving ability', 'singing ability',
'remembering jokes', 'giving a presentation', 'changing self', 'keeping healthy'

After each of these, ask one or two people standing towards the 'terrible' end why they have rated themselves in this position. Explore any self-perception of their ability using the following questions:

■ Who told you that you were not very good at this?

■ What do you tell yourself when you think about this skill?

Use similar questions to explore the self-perceptions of those positioned towards the other end of the scale.

▶

ACTIVITY 7.2 *Continued*

Key points

- It will often become apparent that a significant adult 'told' us (or gave a message that we interpreted in this way) early on that we were not good/should be better at particular skills. Self-image is founded on the feedback we get about ourselves, and the 'ideal self' is founded on what we believe others think we should be. Ask participants to reflect for a moment on the messages they heard or intuited from their parents — what echoes do these leave within us even now? ('It is selfish to put yourself before others', 'Nothing but the best is good enough'.) A great deal of these messages will be meshed into our overall 'ideal self', and not living up to them can leave us feeling inadequate or uncomfortable many years later, even when we do not consciously believe them anymore.

Give out Resource Sheet 26: The cycle of low self-esteem, and talk through the following key points:

- If we encounter a degree of failure or find something difficult, the messages about 'what we are like' can become internalised. We tell ourselves 'I'm no good at this.' This self-talk reinforces the beliefs.

- Because we often stop trying when we believe we are 'no good' ('There's no point: I'll only get it wrong.') we don't get the practice that would help us to improve and therefore the reality begins to accord with our belief.

- In order to change our beliefs about ourselves we need to reinforce the new message many times, in a way that we feel is true. If we believe we will perform well in an area, we need little reinforcement — but if we believe we will fail, we will need a lot more to 'extinguish' the old learning. One way to do this is by changing our 'self-talk', the focus of the final section of this module.

Supporting pupils in developing an accurate and positive self-image

As self-image is learnt, it can be changed. Achieving a realistic and positive self-image depends crucially on self-awareness.

ACTIVITY 7.3: Developing self-awareness and valuing ourselves   **10 minutes**

Ask participants to thoughtshower the different areas of self-awareness that we can help children to develop in the educational context and flipchart responses. Examples might include:

- understanding their feelings, thoughts and behaviours (refer to Module 2)

- understanding their learning style (visual, auditory or kinaesthetic — refer to Module 6)

- knowing their skills and abilities, gifts and talents

- gaining knowledge in 'how they are smart' — that is, their particular type of intelligence (see Module 6).

In addition to these areas of personal knowledge and understanding, children also need to hear some key messages (which will come from the environment and especially from recognising what important adults do). Some helpful messages are:

- we are all unique and valuable

- while there are many similarities between people, there are also differences and this is to be celebrated

ACTIVITY 7.3 *Continued*

- all 'intelligences' are equally valuable

- we all have good and less good habits — no-one is perfect

- we can all change and get better — nothing is 'fixed'.

Ask participants to spend a few minutes reflecting on, and sharing, how these values are transmitted and reinforced both explicitly and through the environment. What other similar values are promoted?

ACTIVITY 7.4: Developing self-awareness and valuing through 'Golden moments'   15 minutes

Ask participants to work in pairs, and explain that one person will listen while the other talks for two or three minutes about something they have done which they feel proud of. It might be something personal — say decorating a bathroom — or professional, for example, coping with a confrontation. Remind them about the importance of 'active listening' (see Module 1 pp. xxx–xxx).

The role of the listener is to focus on the skills, qualities and talents that their partner demonstrated in their achievement; they can encourage the speaker but must take care not to become drawn into the conversation. Listeners can be invited to take notes if they wish. The skills they notice might include persistence, kindness, the ability to delay gratification, seeing something from someone else's point of view, managing frustration. When the speaker has finished, the listener's role is to spend one minute feeding back the qualities, talents and skills that they noticed, attaching each one to a specific example — 'I thought you showed great persistence when you … '.

When both have had a turn as speaker and listener, ask participants to sum up how they felt in response to the activity.

Key points
- We are often unaware of our skills and abilities, and/or take them for granted. It is important to hear messages from others, and experience positive feedback.

- Our tendency is to focus on what we do wrong, rather than what we have done well, and it is rare in a professional context that we have any opportunity to share the latter.

- The specificity of the praise we receive in this activity is important — we are more able to believe positive feedback when specific examples are given. This is also vital when using praise to build pupils' self-esteem.

ACTIVITY 7.5: The power of language   5 minutes

We can encourage others to value themselves, and to develop feelings of self-efficacy, competence, confidence and optimism through the language we use, and the language we encourage them to use (both out loud and in their self-talk). Remind participants of the links between thoughts, feelings and behaviours (see Module 2 pp. 47–49) and explain that what we tell ourselves (our thoughts) will lead to emotional responses.

ACTIVITY 7.5 *Continued*

Catherine Corrie (2003) writes about the effect of the language we use (to ourselves and others) on our feelings about ourselves. Pessimistic thinking, she says, makes our failures or difficulties feel and sound

- permanent ('I can't do maths'.)

- global ('I can never do anything right'.)

- the result of something lacking in us ('I'm too stupid to understand this'.)

The strategy for promoting optimistic thinking is to challenge the implications of such statements, rephrasing them in a way that redefines the problem in terms that are

- temporary ('You can't do this sort of addition yet'.)

- specific ('What specifically do you think you haven't done right'?)

- solvable by the provision of a missing ingredient ('You are having difficulty with this because you haven't been taught what to do yet'. 'When you practise a little more, you will begin to find it much easier'.)

Ask participants to think of some examples of pessimistic talk that they or the pupils they work with use. How could these be rephrased?

Intersessional focus

Participants should focus on the use of positive feedback with pupils (ad hoc or structured 'Golden Moments') and be ready to feed back any effects they notice.

Alternatively, note down the statements that a) they themselves or b) pupils make that demonstrate pessimistic thinking, and challenge these in the ways suggested in Activity 7.4.

N.B. Staff should be given an opportunity to feed back on the intersessional focus in the way agreed.

Resource Sheet 25: Pre-session task

Reading: The importance of self-esteem

Self-esteem, self-concept, self-confidence, self-image — there are many words that people use to describe the way we see or feel about others and the way we see ourselves. You will have come across one model in Module 2 (see pp. 52–64) which suggests that there are three components to self-esteem; a sense of acceptable self; a sense of belonging, and a sense of personal power (that is, the belief that we have the power to make a difference). Module 7 offers an opportunity to explore the meaning of self-esteem — the value that we place upon ourselves.

Whether this value is high or low relates, among other things, to the distance between our 'self-image' (what we believe ourselves to be like) and our 'ideal self' (what we believe we should be like, or would want to be like) and this is explored more fully in the session.

When we have a good self-image (when we can identify good things about ourselves and accept the things we are not so good at) and a realistic ideal self (when our expectations are not impossibly high), the difference between the two is not great and we will rate our value highly. This contributes, alongside our feelings of belonging and self-efficacy, to sound self-esteem.

When we have a negative self-image (when we can only focus on the 'bad' things about ourselves) and/or an unrealistic ideal self (perhaps resulting from other people's expectations of us), the difference between them is great, and the value we place on ourselves is low. This contributes (again, in conjunction with our feelings of belonging and self-efficacy) to low self-esteem.

Self-esteem (or whatever words we use to describe how we view ourselves) is fundamentally important for schools as it exerts possibly the most significant effect on our behaviour, our expectations of ourselves and others, our willingness to try new tasks or to take risks and on the feelings, thoughts and behaviours that result.

Links between self-esteem and emotional literacy

There is a two-way relationship between self-esteem and emotional literacy. Firstly, anything we do to develop self-awareness will also support the development of a realistic self-image, a key aspect of self-esteem. Learners' sense of belonging will be encouraged by an emotionally literate ethos and structures, and work on 'locus of control' (see Module 6 pp. 99–100) and responsibility will encourage feelings of personal power.

In turn, much of our motivation to learn and use social, emotional and behavioural skills depends on us having a strong sense of self or sound self-esteem. For example, we can learn the skills of assertiveness but if we do not value ourselves we will not put the knowledge into practice, believing that we don't deserve the same rights we accord others. Similarly we can learn strategies for fair conflict resolution, but if we don't value ourselves we will deny our own needs and interests and make decisions that are not in our best interests.

Our self-esteem also fundamentally affects how well we learn, our motivation, persistence and resilience (see Module 6 pp. 95–105). If we believe we cannot influence outcomes or events, we will not be interested in using strategies for developing persistence and resilience, and we will lack the motivation even to begin to set and strive for our goals. If we rate our value poorly, we will believe from the start that we won't achieve the desired end.

Before the session, reflect on the 'money in the pocket' metaphor used by Maines and Robinson (1999).

'Children come to you with different levels of self-concept and those with high self-concept are likely to achieve the best results. We can make the comparison with money; those with most money in their pockets can take risks, try new things, afford to risk a little and even if they lose some they are not poor. The child with low self-concept is like a child with very little money. He can't afford to gamble because he runs the risk of failing and being left with nothing at all. So it is up to you to support, encourage and protect the child with low self-concept … . (pp. 9–10)'

Resource Sheet 26: The cycle of low self-esteem

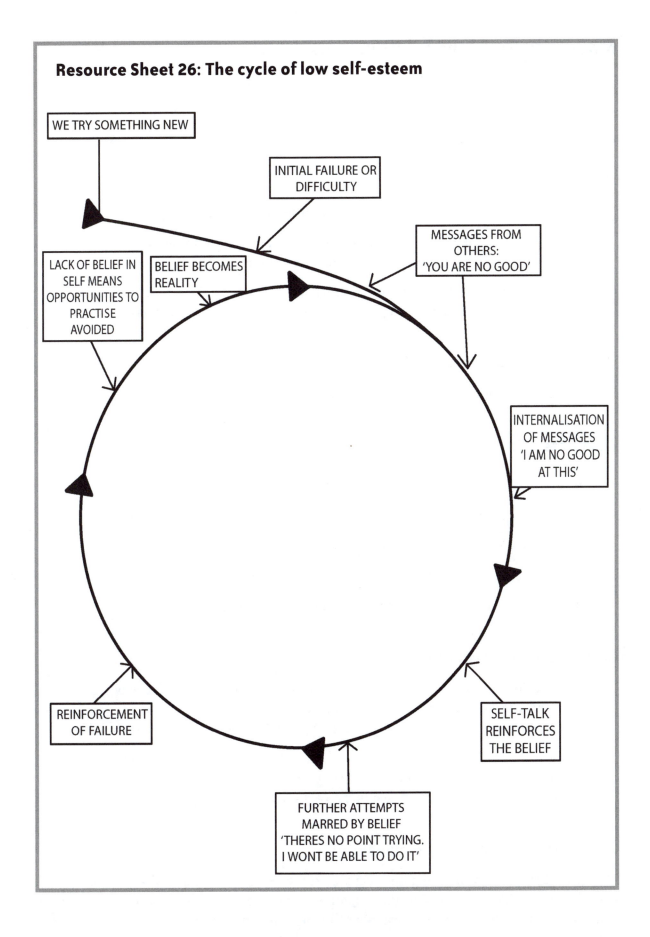

Module 8: Handling relationships

Suggested timing of session: April Year 2

Aims and learning intentions

Staff will

- be familiar with the broad development of social and relationship skills

- be clear about the skills, knowledge and understanding we are seeking to develop and the prerequisite underpinnings of these

- have a clear idea about how the organization can support the development of these skills through both 'taught' and 'caught' (environmental) aspects.

Underpinning concepts and theory

- The development of SEBS pt. 5 – social skills.

Resources

- Resource Sheet 27: Pre-session task – The story of Sam

- Resource Sheet 28: A visualisation

- Resource Sheet 29: A checklist of social skills

- Resource Sheet 30: How do we do it?

- Resource Sheet 31: Relationship management – My profile

Useful additional resources

- BBC Video/DVD (2005) *Social, emotional and behavioural skills.* The following three dramas deal specifically with social issues: Programme 4: 2 Tough Crew; Programme 5: Good to be bad, Hard to be good; Programme 6: Fool and the gang.

- *Supporting SEAL: Social and Emotional Aspects of Learning.* A set of assembly stories, stimulus stories and whole-school resources to promote a whole-school ethos for developing emotional literacy (Futurelink Publishing, 2005).

Links to DfES primary SEAL materials

Theme 2: 'Getting on and falling out' focuses on the skills of making and sustaining friendships. Theme 6: 'Relationships' further explores friendships, including break-ups and social issues such as peer pressure and stereotyping. Theme 3: 'Bullying' offers a focused application of many of the relationship management issues raised, and an important opportunity to tackle this fundamental social and emotional issue.

Pre-session task

Give out *Resource Sheet 27: Pre-Session task* and ask participants to read the case study and bring completed answers to the two questions to the Module 8 session.

Suggested activities – facilitator's notes

The development of SEBS – social skills   5 minutes

Introduce the topic for the session with the following key points to link the area to what has been covered in previous modules:

- Social skills or 'interpersonal intelligence' (Gardner, 1983) are essential to success in life (Goleman, 1998).

- Our social nature is motivated by our need to belong. Remind participants of the importance of 'belonging' as a motivator for behaviour in Maslow's Hierarchy (see Module 1 p. 50). The need is strong, and most staff will be familiar with those pupils who will do almost anything in order to belong – hence the power of 'peer pressure'.

- As with other SEBS, social competencies are both developmentally hard-wired and dependent on environmental context and sociocultural influences. Babies demonstrate social smiling early on, enjoy playing peekaboo and waving by 1-year-old. By three-years-old most are able to take turns in simple games. Between nine-years-old and adolescence the adoption of a 'cool emotional front' signals another development in social maturity. It is at this point that a peer group becomes the most important reference point for social comparison, and from adolescence onwards young people adopt a range of sophisticated self-presentation strategies.

ACTIVITY 8.1: What social skills should we be helping children to develop?   15 minutes

Divide the group into two groups, A and B, and give each a flipchart and some felt-pens. Invite both groups to relax and to close their eyes. When they are relaxed read them the visualisation and instructions from Resource Sheet 28.

After an appropriate length of time ask participants to open their eyes and use the flipchart to record together (pictorially or in a list) what they saw and heard. Set a time limit of five minutes, and then use the posters or lists to agree on the social and relationship skills we would support children in acquiring in a 'perfect classroom'. This could represent an overall list of social skills we would like children or young people to have at the end of KS1/3' and so on, or a roughly developmental picture. Resource Sheet 29: A checklist of social skills could be used as a resource for further discussion or exploration, if time is available.

Key points
- People can use good social skills for positive or negative purposes, for example in using them to manipulate others. There is, therefore, a value (and cultural) dimension to helping pupils develop social skills that we need to be aware of. We must be alert to our own biases and cultural assumptions and ensure we are not imposing our view on others, but rather work together within a framework of universal rights and responsibilities.

ACTIVITY 8.2: The prerequisites of developing social skills   **10 minutes**

Refer participants to the first question posed as part of the pre-session task, reminding participants of the key elements of the case study as appropriate. Discuss responses and add any skills to the list generated in Activity 8.1.

Key points

■ The case study illustrates the subtlety and sophistication of many socially-based skills. For example, it highlights the following: the fact that we have unspoken rules of interaction; the importance of noticing and responding to emotional and interpersonal cues; the need to be sensitive to the social hierarchies that exist.

■ Socially skilled children and adults seem to pick up these subtle social abilities — when joining a group, for example, skilled individuals will watch, catch the emotional tone and deliberately keep to 'the way things are done'.

Ask participants to share the measures they identified in the second question of the task, and record responses.

Key points

■ Because of the subtle nature of many social skills and understanding, programmes which focus on 'behavioural' change and developing purely 'social' skills in isolation from knowledge and understanding in the other key domains of emotional literacy on which social skills depend are often less successful.

■ Remind participants of the model of the key domains of emotional literacy from Module 2, in which self-awareness, empathy and managing feelings are seen to underlie social skills.

Supporting the development of social skills

ACTIVITY 8.3: Application to pupil contexts   **15 minutes**

Give out Resource Sheet 30: How do we do it? Ask participants to consider each of the listed skills, knowledge and understandings underlying the development of social skills, and to explore in groups how their school facilitates the development of each. Share feedback. The SLT might like to use this information, in conjunction with the list constructed in Activity 8.1, as the basis of curriculum planning in this area (if they are not already using a programme).

Intersessional focus

Ask staff working individually or in pairs to take a skill area from the list generated in Activity 8.1 (for example, assertive communication or problem-solving) and consider what provision is made ('taught and caught') to develop pupils' skills in this area and how the area could be further developed at a classroom and whole-school level.

A further activity is to complete the personal profile in the area of relationship management (Resource Sheet 31). An interpretation guide is included, and participants should be reminded of the guidelines in completing it, and the need to transfer their scores to the scoring grid (see Chapter 2 p. 24 and 26 respectively).

N.B. Staff should be given an opportunity to feed back on the intersessional focus in the way agreed.

Resource Sheet 27: Pre-session task

The story of Sam – A case study

Read the following case study and consider what SEBS Sam needs to develop. Include any skills, knowledge and understanding in the key domains of self-awareness and empathy as well as specifically social skills.

What would you do for Sam? List five things that you would do or areas that you would focus on to support him.

Sam joined my Year 6 class half way through the Autumn term. At first things seemed to go very well; the children in the class were interested in him and keen to work and play with him. From my perspective he seemed bright and participated well in lessons.

Things soon started to go wrong however. The children didn't want to sit or work with Sam, and he seemed increasingly isolated in the playground. I talked to a few of the children and they reported finding him 'irritating' and 'annoying', although they could not specify anything in particular that he did to upset them.

After two weeks his mother came to see me. She told me that Sam wasn't keen to come to school, that he felt that the other children didn't like him. He was unhappy and bewildered by this. We both felt puzzled as Sam had started so well, he wasn't aggressive or unkind, he didn't boast and he shared his things. I agreed to carry out some observations over the next week to see if they would throw any light on the situation, and to talk to the children in a circle time (with Sam's agreement), about how he was feeling and what we could all do to help him to feel welcomed and included. We had a successful circle time in which children offered to invite him to their houses, include him in games and agreed to work with him. I felt confident that this would solve the problem …

However, the observations were interesting – while Sam didn't do anything deliberately provocative, I began to see some patterns in his social interactions that concerned me. These are some of the things I observed:

- Sam seemed to 'get it wrong' a lot in casual conversations and to respond to casual enquiries in great detail, or alternatively to make monosyllabic, factual answers, often invading the personal space of others.

- He didn't seem to know how or when to end a conversation, and would keep talking in the face of obvious signs of disinterest or others' attempts to 'move the conversation on'.

- He would often walk up to a group of children who were chatting and as soon as possible start talking himself – often about a different subject.

- While in the playground I observed Sam join in with a group of boys playing football. Soon after he started playing he disagreed with a decision that would have favoured a popular boy, and persisted with stating his point of view until the boy said 'Whatever' and play continued. Sam seemed to have elected himself unofficial 'captain' and within ten minutes had 'helped' three players by pointing out where they were going wrong! It was clear to me that the boys were beginning to have trouble containing their irritation, and the game soon disintegrated.

Resource Sheet 28: A visualisation

Imagine that you are entering a school. You walk slowly down a long corridor with two doors at the end. If you are in Group A you open the left-hand door, and if Group B the right-hand door. You each enter into an empty classroom set up for your particular age group and you sit yourself down at the back of the classroom, covering yourself with a magic cloak of invisibility that seems to have been left for you only. As pupils begin to arrive, if you are in Group A you observe a classroom in which all the adults and pupils are superbly socially skilled, while if you are in Group B you observe a very different picture — in this classroom both pupils and adults demonstrate no social skills whatsoever.

Ask participants to focus on this scene for one or two minutes to notice what they can see, what they can hear, how it feels to be in the room. Ask them to follow the children out of the classroom into the corridors and onto the playground or into the dinner hall — what sort of things are going on? What can they see and hear?

Resource Sheet 29: A checklist of social skills

This list is not exhaustive or comprehensive, but a starting point for schools:

— solve disagreements and problems peacefully with friends and others

— have good relationships

— do things for others

— use 'push-ups' (compliments) and avoid using put-downs

— listen to each other

— cooperate (working or playing together to successfully complete a task or achieve a goal in a fair way)

— problem-solve taking into account what each person wants

— know how the other person is feeling and help them to feel better or share excitement/joy/happiness

— be reliable, honest and trustworthy

— join in with other children's activities

— cope with rejection

— use assertive communication

— play in teams, take turns, share

— compete fairly, maintaining respect for others, sound self-esteem and winning or losing with dignity

— show an interest in other people

— know how to look and act in a friendly way

— know how to start and continue a conversation

— speak appropriately to different people

— don't use stereotypes but value diversity, show respect and interest in others, enjoy finding out about different people

— recognize and resist or harness peer pressure where appropriate.

Resource Sheet 30: How do we do it?

	In order to make and sustain positive relationships and resist negative social pressures (e.g. stereotyping) we need:	How do we do it? Environmental factors (including adult modelling and whole school strategies)	How do we do it? Through the 'taught' curriculum – SEBS, PSHE, RE, Assemblies, the curriculum etc.
Self-awareness and self-valuing:	To recognize emotions and the way we work in order to be able to understand this in others		
	To be aware of our own behaviour and emotional displays and the effect of these on others		
	To recognize and own our feelings, and not to put the blame on others ('He made me do it')		
	To recognize and value our own needs in a situation, as well as those of other people		
	To know and accept ourselves, know that we belong and believe in our power to make a difference		
Managing our feelings:	To manage our own emotions and needs in order to help us make good decisions		
	To manage our emotions creatively and healthily if we chose to put our emotional needs to one side to focus on another person's emotions or needs		
	To respond appropriately and politely to others while still recognizing our own feelings, for example, responding both politely and honestly when someone gives a present		

This page can be photocopied. © *Developing Emotionally Literate Staff*, Morris and Casey, 2006

	In order to make and sustain positive relationships and resist negative social pressures (e.g. stereotyping) we need:	How do we do it? Environmental factors (including adult modelling and whole school strategies)	How do we do it? Through the 'taught' curriculum – SEBS, PSHE, RE, Assemblies, the curriculum etc.
Empathy:	To understand that: ■ other people can have the same feelings as us although they might be aroused and displayed in different ways ■ what we do impacts on others' feelings and emotions ■ people's behaviour is linked to their thoughts and feelings		
	To read others emotional signals including non-verbal ones		
	To put ourselves in another's shoes (take a different perspective)		
	To respond in ways that make others feel good, e.g. using 'push-ups' (compliments) instead of 'put-downs', and using active listening skills (see Module 1)		

Above all, in order to engage in a socially based world, we need to have a positive and welcoming attitude to diversity, to recognize our common humanity while valuing and celebrating the ways in which we ourselves and others are unique individuals.

This page can be photocopied. © *Developing Emotionally Literate Staff*, Morris and Casey, 2006

Resource Sheet 31: Relationship management – my profile

To what extent are the following true of you?

Very True – This is how I feel/think/act

Quite True – This is quite often true of me and would be recognizable to other people.

Seldom True – I don't often think/feel/act like this

Never true/not true – I don't think/feel/act like this

Relationship management questions	Very True	Quite True	Seldom True	Never True		
I feel uncomfortable when someone gets too close to me emotionally	0	1	2	3	△	20–24
I have several friends I can count on in times of trouble	3	2	1	0	△	16–19
I show a lot of love and affection to my friends/family	3	2	1	0	△	12–15
I doubt if my colleagues really care about me as a person	0	1	2	3	△	8–11
I have a difficult time making friends	0	1	2	3	△	4–7
There are some people I 'connect with' at a deeper level	3	2	1	0	△	0–3
I have deeply loved another person	3	2	1	0		
I am able to make a long-term commitment to a relationship.	3	2	1	0		
TOTAL						
GRAND TOTAL						

Conflict management questions	Very True	Quite True	Seldom True	Never True
I would not express my feelings if I believed they would cause a diasagreement	0	1	2	3
I remain calm even in situations when others get angry	3	2	1	0
I think that it is better not to stir up problems if you can avoid it	0	1	2	3
I have a hard time getting agreement from my team	0	1	2	3
I ask for feedback from my peers on my performance	3	2	1	0
I am good at organizing and motivating groups of people	3	2	1	0
When I make critical comment I focus on the behaviour and not the person	3	2	1	0
I rarely have the urge to tell someone off	0	1	2	3
I'm often asked to help out when people are at loggerheads	3	2	1	0
TOTAL				
GRAND TOTAL				

△ 25–27
△ 20–24
△ 15–19
△ 10–14
△ 5–9
△ 0–4

This section is about skills and competence in making and maintaining good relationships. Being able to connect and share with others is as important as being able to resolve conflicts when they arise between you and another person.

This page can be photocopied. © *Developing Emotionally Literate Staff*, Morris and Casey, 2006

RELATIONSHIP MANAGEMENT

Definition: The Relationship Management scale measures how well you create and sustain a network of people with whom you are honest and open. The opposite end of this scale is isolation: an inability to create a network that sustains and supports you.

Changing and developing

List the people you are 'yourself' with.

Notice what emotions and experiences you are most comfortable talking about.

Experiment with sharing something a little outside your comfort zone with a person you trust.

CONFLICT MANAGEMENT

Definition: Conflict management explores your ability to stay calm, focused and emotionally grounded, even in the face of disagreement or conflict. It involves finding ways to create win—wins where both people feel valued.

Changing and developing

Prior to a meeting in which you will need to express your position, reflect on which elements are essential for you.

Focus on the comments being conveyed, not the person delivering them.

Remind yourself to remain open and receptive to differing points of view when you feel yourself tensing up and resisting. You don't have to agree or go along with it — only be open.

Module 9: Dealing with difficult feelings

Suggested timing of session: May Year 2

Aims and learning intentions

Staff will

- understand the impact of development and cultural variations on the 'social emotions' of jealousy, guilt, embarrassment and so on

- be familiar with a range of strategies for managing these difficult feelings

- have revised using a problem-solving tool in relation to dealing with difficult feelings.

Underpinning concepts and theory

- the development of SEBS pt. 6 – the 'social' emotions (jealousy, guilt and embarrassment)

- understanding how 'cognitive distortions' affect feelings and behaviour

- problem-solving models

Resources

- Resource Sheet 32: Pre-session task

- Resource Sheet 33: The development of the 'social' emotions

- Resource Sheet 34: Dealing with feelings – A strategy.

Useful additional resources

- BBC Video/DVD (2005) Social, emotional and behavioural skills (Programme 4: 2 Tough Crew; Programme 5: Good to be bad, Hard to be good; Programme 6: Fool and the gang).

- *Supporting SEAL: Social and Emotional Aspects of Learning.* A set of assembly stories, stimulus stories and whole-school resources to promote a whole-school ethos for developing emotional literacy (Futurelink Publishing, 2005).

Links to DfES primary SEAL materials

Theme 6: Relationships explores a range of 'social' feelings within the context of our important relationships, including family and friends.

Pre-session task

Give participants a copy of *Resource Sheet 32: Pre-session task*. Ask them to read the story 'Guilty!' and to carry out the associated tasks, ready for use in the staff session for Module 9.

Suggested activities – facilitator's notes

The development of the 'social' emotions

ACTIVITY 9.1: Our experiences	15 minutes

Prior to the session put up five flipcharts labelled 'guilt', 'jealousy', 'embarrassment' and two unlabelled. Divide each sheet into the number of year groups taught in the school, and label each with a year group. Invite participants to place their Post-it™, completed as part of the pre-session task, in the appropriate place on the flipcharts, and to record their rating for how much of a problem the focus emotion causes in their classroom or context.

Offer participants five minutes to read through the sheet, noting down any changes or patterns they notice specific to age groups; for example, jealousy of friendships (as opposed to possessions) often becomes an issue as children progress through KS2 (the 'threesome problem'), and embarrassment becomes more acute as children approach adolescence and as the peer group becomes the most significant point of social reference. Take brief feedback (perhaps one point per participant).

ACTIVITY 9.2: The background	10 minutes

Give out Resource Sheet 33: The development of the 'social emotions' and talk through the following key points.

Key points
■ Remind participants about previous work done on the development of emotions – what we feel, how much we feel it, how we show it and how we respond to it all depend on the two factors: individual disposition and life experiences, environment and culture.

What we feel in response to different situations changes over the course of development

Ask participants to answer the quiz question on Resource Sheet 33.

The answer is that the younger child is likely to answer 'the first boy', while the older child is likely to answer 'the second boy'. This is because the stimuli for feelings of guilt change as we get older. Before the age of about eight-years-old, guilt is related primarily to outcome. After this age children begin to see guilt in relation to intention.

■ The situations that result in us feeling guilty, jealous or embarrassed vary according to cultural norms

Although guilt, jealousy and embarrassment are found universally, what elicits them is often culturally dependent.

A good example of cultural relativity is the research of Miller and Bersoff (1992). They worked with American and Indian subjects, finding out what sort of behaviours were thought to be more unaccept-

ACTIVITY 9.2 *Continued*

able (and therefore likely to induce guilt); breaking a social obligation (for example, failing to deliver the rings to a best friend's wedding) **or** committing a breach of the law, such as stealing a train ticket to get to the wedding.

There were interesting differences – the Indian subjects would feel less guilty about stealing the train ticket than failing to deliver the wedding rings, while the pattern was reversed for the Americans.

This is a common difference between the 'individualist' culture of many Western cultures, and the collectivist cultures more typical of Eastern and African cultures.

■ These emotions are complex and often experienced as a 'cluster' of uncomfortable feelings

Refer participants to the Pre-session Task question 1, and ask them to share the clusters of feelings that they associated with each emotion. Flipchart the responses. These might include:

– guilt – anxious, regretful, remorseful

– embarrassment – upset, angry, uncertain, at a loss

– jealousy – angry, inadequate, vulnerable, indignant

– shame – humiliated, despairing, self-disgusted.

■ Emotions are a 'spur to action' – what might these 'difficult' emotions be telling us?

'Emotion' comes from the Latin word meaning to move (emotion, motion) and one of its key functions is to precipitate action – when we experience an uncomfortable feeling we are motivated to do something about it so that we feel better.

Managing difficult feelings
ACTIVITY 9.3: Dealing with difficult feelings   15 minutes

In the round (using the rules for circle time) ask participants to draw on their responses to the Pre-session Task question 3 in completing the following sentence:

'When I feel (choose: embarrassed, guilty, jealous, ashamed) I find it helps me to...'
Ask someone to act as scribe to record the strategies.

Give out Resource Sheet 34: Dealing with feelings – A strategy and ask participants to link the strategies they have identified with the process outlined. Explore how this might work for them and how it could be adapted for sharing with pupils.

■ Identify the feeling (see Resource Sheet 7 from Module 2 for information on helping pupils to recognize and label feelings).

■ Own and accept the feeling: A key strategy in helping children to own their feelings, is to teach them to use 'I' messages rather than 'you' messages. Maines and Robinson (1999) use the example, 'I feel lonely when you don't ask me to play. I would like you to ask me to join in' rather than 'You are all ignoring me'. Encourage children to say 'I feel ... when ... And what I would like is ... '

One really important message to get across to everyone is that it is OK and normal to experience a whole range of emotions – even when they feel uncomfortable. If we are told that some emotions are

▶

127

ACTIVITY 9.3: *Continued*

'bad' and 'You shouldn't feel like that', we equate experiencing that emotion with being a bad person. This can lead us to deny we have it or to try to mask it with another emotion (often anger).

■ Ask 'Am I worrying rather than trying to solve a problem'?

Worrying is when our thoughts go round in circles without moving us on. Explain that when we worry we often

– focus on the problem, not the solution

– imagine the very worst outcome

– magnify its importance

– catastrophize ('If I don't pass this test, they'll fire me, then I won't be able to pay the rent, and I'll lose the house and....')

– think only in terms of 'all or nothing'

– label and judge the person (often ourselves) rather than the behaviour.

Participants may have met the idea of these 'cognitive distortions' if they have come across 'cognitive behavioural therapy' (CBT). Ask participants to read through the challenges on the resource sheet and relate them to any strategies they use.

■ Problem-solve

Remind participants of the importance of having a consistent strategy within the school for supporting pupils in solving problems. The four key steps are:

1 Make sure you are calm (the 'ready' stage in the DfES SEAL materials; 'stop' in the 'stop – think – do' model; 'red' in the traffic lights model).

2 Think it through (the 'steady', 'think' or 'amber' stage) generating solutions, weighing them up and considering consequences and so on.

3 Put it into action ('go', 'do', 'green').

4 The 'replay' stage at a later time where you consider what went well, what you would change and what you have learnt. This is essential in helping young people to get know themselves, link cause and effect and consolidate their learning, using it to plan for the future.

ACTIVITY 9.4: Applying the learning   15 minutes

Ask participants to use the resource sheet to consider the events in the 'Guilty!' story (Resource Sheet 32), 'mapping' the various events in the story to each of the stages in the 'dealing with feeling' strategy. Alternatively, they may wish to try out the strategy on a personal or professional situation.

Intersessional focus

Ask participants to focus on supporting pupils in managing these difficult feelings, maybe trying out – if appropriate – some of the activities in the classroom and sharing strategies (their own and the pupils'). Alternatively, they might prefer to feedback on how they have used or adapted the strategy themselves.

Resource Sheet 32: Pre-session task

Guilty!

Martin doesn't really do romantic gestures, which is why it was so wonderful when, out of the blue, he brought home a ring he'd had specially made for me; diamond and opals set in white gold. It was beautiful. I loved it mostly because he had bought it for me, but, if I'm honest, also because it was the single most expensive thing I had ever owned. I wore it every day ... until the moment last week when I looked down at my hand and suddenly realized it was gone. I couldn't believe it. My heart lurched and a feeling of panic came over me. My beautiful ring, where could it be? Then I remembered noticing a little crack in the band at the back the week before. Why hadn't I taken it to the jewellers there and then? What on earth was I going to do now?

Every time I caught sight of my bare hand I felt a wave of guilt wash over me — anxiety, shame, anger at myself, and above all a feeling of sickening dread when I thought about having to tell Martin. I went over and over it in my head — how could I have risked losing something so precious? Why had I been so stupid? Why hadn't I taken it to the jewellers while I had the chance? At night I lay awake as my thoughts spiralled out of control.

So I did what I suppose we all do when difficult, unpleasant thoughts make us feel bad — I tried to blot them out. Whenever they popped up I would quickly push them down and try to ignore them. I attempted to make myself feel better by thinking that maybe it would turn up, maybe someone would find it and return it, things might be OK.

But it was no good. At last I felt so bad I realized I would have to talk to someone. I chose Mia because she's a good friend and she listens. I poured it all out to her.

'I really loved that ring,' I wailed, 'not just because it was such a lovely gift but because it was so gorgeous.' I wondered if she'd think I was materialistic. But she just listened sympathetically, so I went on, 'and I know I should have got it mended when I saw the crack. That makes me feel that I was lazy — that I just didn't care enough as well as being so careless.' Mia squeezed my hand. 'And what will he say when I tell him I've lost his ring?' I cried, 'what will he think of me?'

Strangely enough just talking to Mia helped to sort out what was actually making me feel so bad. We began to unravel the threads of what had just felt like a mess of tangled emotions, and she helped me to see how I could tackle each bit of the problem independently. We practised what I would say to Martin if the ring didn't turn up. I faced up to the fact that even if he was angry with me, this would be understandable. I would just have to apologize and explain what had happened, remembering that I wasn't the worst person in the world, just someone who had made a mistake.

Talking to Mia helped me put the whole episode in proportion. What had happened was a shame, but not a major tragedy. When she asked me if I'd had a really good search in the house for it, I realized that I'd spent so much time worrying, I hadn't actually had a thorough, methodical look in the places it was most likely to be. I couldn't wait to get home.

I found it under the cat's litter tray. What a relief. It was wonderful to have the ring back but it was good to know as well that I'd learned a few lessons I wouldn't forget in a hurry.

The Tasks

1 Guilt, jealousy, resentment, embarrassment — these are all emotions that go along with the fundamentally social nature of human beings. Experiencing them is part and parcel of having relationships with other people. Most of them involve a cluster of feelings rather than just one. Write down any feelings that form part of each of these emotions for you, each on a sticky note for use in the module.

2 Consider any strategies you use when you experience one of these difficult feelings to make yourself feel better.

3 Review (and note down if you wish) what typically elicits these feelings in the pupils you teach. Try to think of a recent example of each feeling from your work with pupils to share during the session.

4 Rate each emotion in terms of the degree of unrest/difficulty/disruption it causes to the class or group (with 0 as 'Never a problem' and 10 representing 'One of the biggest issues in the class'), and be prepared to share your rating and the reasons for it in the session.

Resource Sheet 33: The development of the 'social' emotions

What we feel in response to different situations changes over the course of development.

QUIZ

If you outline the following scenarios to two children, one aged five and one aged eight, and ask which person has been naughtiest, what do you anticipate each child will answer?

1   A boy is playing in his room and accidentally tears a great big hole in his new curtains.

2   A boy is in his room, finds a pair of scissors and cuts a tiny hole in his new curtains, because he is cross with his mum.

The situations that invite us to feel guilty, jealous or embarrassed vary according to cultural norms.

'Although people of different cultures can sometimes agree on the types of situations that lead to emotions like happiness, sadness, and fear, there are also culture-specific links between situations and emotion. This is principally because our emotional reactions depend on highly subjective interpretations of events, which themselves may reflect particular sociocultural norms and circumstances'. DfES, 2005, p. 61

These emotions are complex and often experienced as a 'cluster' of uncomfortable feelings.

Emotions are a 'spur to action' — what might these 'difficult' emotions be telling us?

Resource Sheet 34: Dealing with feelings – a strategy

■ Identify the feeling

■ Own and accept the feeling

■ Ask 'What is this feeling telling me?' Use the feeling to identify the problem.

■ Ask 'Am I worrying rather than trying to solve a problem?'

■ Challenge your 'faulty thinking'. Ask these questions:

About yourself

— 'Am I being harder on myself than I would be on a friend in my position?'

— 'Am I worrying about or blaming myself for things that I can do nothing about?'

— 'Am I thinking I am a bad person because I have done one or two silly things?'

About the situation

— 'Is there another way of looking at this situation?'

— 'How would I look at this if I was feeling more confident?'

About the outcomes

— 'What is the worst thing that could happen?' ('Would anybody die?' 'Would I go to prison?')

— 'What is the best thing that could happen?'

— 'What is the most likely thing to happen?'

— 'Will it matter in a week/a month/a year?'

■ Problem-solve

Use the four key steps which are:

Calm down

Think it through

Go for it

Review.

Module 10: Change and loss

Note: When working with staff on the effects of change and loss, it is particularly important to maintain ground rules and emotional safety (see Chapter 3). Ensure any special arrangements that might be necessary for members of staff for whom the subject matter might be distressing are agreed prior to the session.

Suggested timing of session: June Year 2

Aims and learning intentions

Staff will

- understand the concept of 'comfort, challenge and stress zones' and how change affects these

- understand the relationship between stress levels and optimum performance

- be familiar with a range of proactive ways in which the school can support pupils in developing strategies for managing change and loss

- know about some common understandings and responses to loss and bereavement (at different ages and stages)

- be clear on where to get further support for themselves and the children, young people and families involved.

Underpinning concepts and theory

- research on transitions and transfer

- 'comfort, challenge and stress zones' in relation to change

- common responses to loss and bereavement.

Resources

- Resource Sheet 35: Pre-session task

- Resource Sheet 36: Comfort, Challenge, Stress zones and Performance.

Links to DfES primary SEAL materials

Loss is covered in Theme 6: Relationships, while the issue of change (including KS2/3 transfer) is covered in Theme 7: Changes.

Useful additional resources and websites

- www.winstonswish.org.uk

- www.Childbereavement.org.uk

- www.childline.org.uk

- www.itsnotyourfault.org (for children whose parents are separating or divorcing)

- *Supporting SEAL: Social and Emotional Aspects of Learning*. A set of assembly stories, stimulus stories and whole-school resources to promote a whole-school ethos for developing emotional literacy (Futurelink Publishing, 2005).

Pre-session task

Give out *Resource Sheet 34* and ask participants to read through and discuss the relevance of the content for the age range of children they each work with. Ask individuals to identify one thing that they have learnt, could put into practice, or would like to follow up from the overview.

Suggested activities – facilitator's notes

Comfort zones, stress, change and loss

ACTIVITY 10.1	5 minutes

Draw a continuum on a flipchart sheet, numbered 0–10. Ask participants to write down two or three changes or losses that pupils might experience with each on a separate Post-it™ note. Ask them to attach these to the continuum at what they consider might be the level of stress that the change or loss they have noted would cause, where 0 is no stress and 10 is the worst possible level of stress.

Ask participants to each contribute one insight they could offer the group about change and loss, elicited by the activity or from personal or professional experiences. The following key points should be included.

Key points

- Life is a series of constant changes, some big, some small, some welcomed and expected, others unexpected and unwelcome.

- Loss is one example of change.

- Bereavement is the most challenging change of all.

- People welcome change to different degrees depending on their disposition and circumstances. (Participants may have rated similar changes at different levels of stress.)

- Change is necessary. Many changes have unanticipated positive outcomes.

- Usually, when something changes, we are supported by other things which stay the same. The most difficult changes are when nothing stays the same (as is often the case for the bereaved, refugees and asylum seekers, and looked-after children).

ACTIVITY 10.2   **10 minutes**

Remind participants of the work they did in Module 1 on the importance of the environment, in particular how difficult it is to perform well when we don't feel that we belong, are valued or have any sort of power or influence over what happens (the three conditions that maintain our self-esteem).

Ask participants to discuss in pairs what other conditions generally need to be met for us to feel within our 'comfort zone'. Take brief feedback.

Key points

The authors' view (in common with many others interested in the area of self-esteem) is that the following elements must be present for us to feel that we are operating within a comfort zone:

- a sense of security and belonging

- a sense of identity (self-valuing)

- a sense of self-efficacy (power)

- a sense of purpose

- a sense of competence.

Ask participants to think of an occasion when they felt within their comfort zone and take feedback on their sense of purpose and competence in this setting.

ACTIVITY 10.3: Application to work with pupils – Changing schools   **20 minutes**

Explain that change and loss make us feel uncomfortable because they can threaten these five 'key conditions' and take us out of our comfort zone.

Ask participants to thoughtshower ideas on how moving to a new school could threaten all five components and record feedback. Ideas might include:

Security: a lack of familiarity with layout; bigger grounds with possible 'danger areas'; don't yet know who can and who can't be trusted.

Belonging: feeling like an outsider; everybody else in groups; don't know adults; loss of old friendship groups.

Purpose: 'role' in new organization not yet clear; yet to find own purpose; academic purposes at odds with social.

Competence and self-efficacy: don't know how things are done or where things are; having to ask for help all the time; new ways of working and new demands (homework; working in IT suites and so on).

Identity/valuing self: change in status from oldest to youngest; need to re-establish place in pecking order.

Give out Resource Sheet 36: Comfort, Challenge, Stress zones and Performance, and talk through the key points.

ACTIVITY 10.3: *Continued*

Key points

- From the graph it is clear that we do not perform at our best when within our comfort zone. So although having a comfort zone is essential for our mental health — a stress-free place which we can retreat to regularly to recharge our batteries and relax — the downside of always operating within it can be boredom, complacency and lack of motivation.

- Note that as stress levels rise so does performance, up to a critical point. This means that when we introduce 'challenge' (carefully pitched to cause the optimum level of stress), we actually perform better. When we experience the level of stress that elicits an optimum level of performance we are often referred to as being within the 'challenge zone'. It retains enough features of the comfort zone to provide a secure base from which to venture forth, but with the addition of challenge both motivation and performance are enhanced.

- However, too much stress lands us in the 'stressed out zone'. This happens when our resources for coping are not adequate for the demands placed upon us — either because the demands are too high, or because our coping resources are for some reason depleted. Under these circumstances we suffer anxiety and may experience an emotional hijack (see Module 2 pp. 52–64), which severely impedes our performance.

Ask participants to relate this to the common and less common changes that children and young people experience identified in the first activity generally, and in relation to transfer in particular.

- Research on transfer and transition points within school reveal significant dips in academic achievement and motivation (Hargreaves and Galton, 2002). These are identified as related to the stress engendered by the process of transfer among other factors.

- One way of conceptualizing the task for schools in supporting children and young people in dealing with change and transfer is to keep them within the 'challenge zone' rather than the 'stressed out zone'. This means that we need to pay attention to increasing pupils' capacity to cope, and ensuring that the demands of change or transfer do not outstrip this capacity.

- Because change and loss are often not planned or expected it is important that support arrangements are not 'bolted on', or set up only as a reaction to a particular incident or an expected change such as transfer to KS3. Arrangements need to be part of a structured and progressive curriculum which aims to develop children's knowledge and understanding in the areas of change and loss, and develops their strategies, skills and emotional resilience for managing change.

Loss and bereavement

There are different levels of working with children and young people in this area. First there is the proactive, structured work where skills, knowledge and understanding about loss and death are built up cumulatively over time; and secondly there is the reactive response to a death or disaster that happens to a pupil, a teacher, in the family of a pupil, or in the community. It is important that schools consider how they will respond in these situations, prior to the event occurring. Proactive, on-going work within the school in this area will make any reactive responses more effective.

ACTIVITY 10.4   **25 minutes**

Explain that many adults working in schools do not feel confident talking to children about death and grief, often seeing it as a specialist field. However, as it is estimated that 'every 30 minutes a child or young person in the UK is bereaved of a parent — that's 55 a day, 20,000 children each year' (Winston's Wish, 2005), it is likely that a great many adults and pupils in schools will be working and socializing with bereaved children. Remind participants of the pre-session reading. Take feedback and explore any issues raised for participants from the reading.

As a group, create a mind-map or thoughtshower of what the organization already addresses in relation to loss and bereavement through the curriculum.

Ask participants to discuss in pairs what they feel it would be useful to know to help them feeling confident about dealing with this issue proactively. The focus needs to be kept on the proactive, structured and progressive build-up of skills, knowledge and understanding in this area, and staff should be referred to the helplines and websites listed for support in dealing with specific instances and crises, or a further staff session should be allocated to this area.

Clearly a short minute activity can do no more than raise awareness of some of the issues involved in helping staff to work proactively with children in the area of loss and bereavement. The SLT might therefore use this session as a springboard for action planning in this area if it is felt appropriate. For schools using the DfES SEAL materials, loss is covered every other year and further training opportunities provided. All staff should be made aware of the sources of support for bereaved families and professionals working with them (see Useful Additional Resources on p. 134).

Resource Sheet 35: Pre-session task

(This text is adapted from Supporting a Bereaved Child or Young Person: A guide for professionals, available to download free from www.winstonswish.org.uk.)

Understanding loss and bereavement – An overview
How age can affect understanding

Our understanding about death and dying increases with age. Broadly speaking, it follows this sort of pattern from three- or four- to around ten-years-old:

- The hamster's not moving but he'll play with me tomorrow.

- The hamster won't ever play again.

- Old people die and we can never play with them again.

- Grandpa may die one day in the future.

- Mummy and Daddy will die when they're old.

- I will die when I'm old.

- Not only old people die. Mummy and Daddy could die tomorrow if something happened.

- I could die tomorrow.

- I can kill myself.

Under the age of five or six, a child may not be able to understand that death is permanent, nor that it happens to every living thing. A four-year-old may be able to tell others confidently that 'my daddy's dead'. However, the next sentence may be: 'I hope he'll be back before my birthday'. or 'He's picking me up tonight'.

Slightly older children may still have this hope and belief that a death will not be permanent but are beginning to understand 'forever'. Children bereaved when they are five- to eight-years-old may feel that they can in some way reverse what has happened ('Dad will come back if I'm very good and eat my broccoli').

They may also feel that they in some way caused a death. ('I was angry with him because he wouldn't fix my bike. It's all my fault').

When first told of a death, younger children may be mainly concerned with the 'when' and 'where' of it. Slightly older ones may also want to know the 'how' and older children and young people will also explore the 'why'.

Younger children will express concerns about their own future: Who will meet me after school? They will need whatever reassurances are possible about continuing everyday activities and arrangements.

As children begin to understand more about death and dying, a death in the family may make them anxious about the health and safety of surviving members. Children may become more clingy or show reluctance to see parents and carers leave. Older children may feel very responsible for their parent(s) and younger siblings, and may feel the need to keep a close eye on their safety.

By the age of ten-years-old, children will usually have all of the bits of the jigsaw puzzle of understanding. They will even understand that they are able to cause their own death. They will appreciate clear and detailed information – beyond 'when', 'where' and 'how' the death happened, they will be interested in 'why'.

Talking about death

When children ask difficult questions, begin by asking: 'What do you think?', and build on their answer.

Younger children may be confused by some of the everyday expressions that people use when someone dies, so it is best to keep language simple and direct. Saying that someone has 'died' or is 'dead' gives a child unique words for a unique event.

Examples of common euphemisms include 'We've lost your mother' (wouldn't you wonder why no-one was out looking everywhere for her?) or 'Granny has gone to sleep', or 'passed away in her sleep' (wouldn't you be scared of going to bed and do all you could to keep yourself and your parents awake at all costs?).

The language surrounding funeral rites can also cause confusion. Children who are asked if they want to see their mother's body have asked 'Why not her head too'?

Families try to convey their beliefs about life after death to their children. It may be best to say something like 'People have all sorts of beliefs about what happens after someone dies. We know that they can't come back and visit us or ring on the phone. Being dead isn't like being in another country. These are some of the things that people believe ... and I believe this ... I wonder what you believe? You may change what you believe as you grow older.'

Responses to bereavement: Feelings, thoughts and behaviour

Children and young people can experience a huge range of feelings and thoughts after the death of someone close. Sometimes people react in unexpected, surprising or even (seemingly) inappropriate ways. Each person will have a unique response — and every reaction is natural.

Some people expect that grief will follow a pattern of response from disbelief and shock through to acceptance. Bereaved young people will tell you that grief is nowhere near as organized or straightforward. Grief feels chaotic. Grief follows no rules. The following list only begins to describe just a few of the responses to the death of someone important to the individual.

■ sadness, not necessarily shown in crying

■ guilt

■ anger towards others and/or the person who has died

■ disbelief

■ confusion

■ fear

■ rage

■ anxiety and a desire to control events and people

■ despair

■ feeling 'frozen'

■ avoiding the subject

■ wanting to keep busy at all costs

■ yearning

■ powerlessness

■ worthlessness.

Resource Sheet 36: Comfort, challenge, stress zones and performance

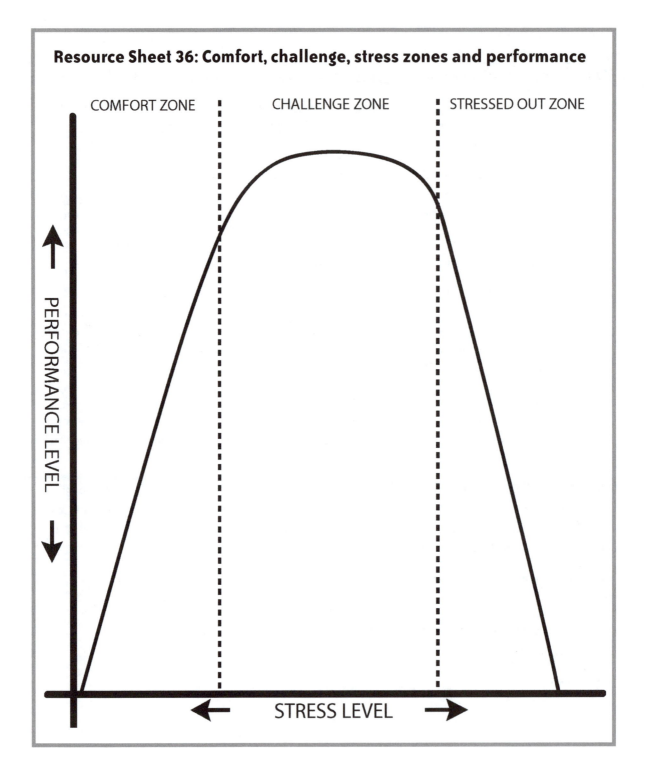

Appendix to Chapter Two

Publications providing emotional literacy profiling tools for children and young people

Developing the Emotionally Literate School by K. Weare, published by Paul Chapman Publishing (2004). This book contains a comprehensive listing of assessment tools and their applications.

Individual Emotional Literacy Indicator (8–15) by Elizabeth Morris and Caroline Scott, published by SEL Publications (2003)

Individual Emotional Literacy Indicator for Young People 16+ by Elizabeth Morris and Caroline Scott, published by SEL Publications (2004)

Class Emotional Literacy Indicator by Elizabeth Morris and Caroline Scott, published by SEL Publications (2003)

Whole School Emotional Literacy Indicator by Elizabeth Morris and Caroline Scott, published by SEL Publications (2003)

Emotional Literacy, Assessment and Intervention by A. Faupal, published by NFER Nelson. (Two are available, one for ages 7–11 and one for ages 11–16)

UK companies offering emotional literacy profiling tools and consultations for adults and schools

School of Emotional Literacy
Contact: **info@schoolofemotional-literacy.com**

Centre for Applied Emotional Intelligence
Contact: **info@emotionalintelligence.com**

Antidote
Contact: **info@antidote.org.uk**

Ei (UK Limited)
Contact: **info@eiworld.org**

SEAL (Society for Effective Affective Learning)
Contact: **seal@seal.org.uk**

A comprehensive list of useful organizations, resources and sources of support can be found in Appendix 9 of the Guidance in the PNS SEAL Resource (DfES), 2005

REFERENCES

Askew, M. and William, D. (1995) *Recent Research in Mathematics Education (OFSTED Reviews of Research)*: Office for Standards in Education. London: The Stationery Office Books.

BBC (2005) *Emotional Literacy: Social, Emotional and Behavioural Skills.* Video Plus Pack/DVD Plus Pack. London: BBC Worldwide Limited (Tel: 0870 830 8000).

Cordingley, P., Bell, M., Rundell, B. and Evans, D. (2003) Centre for the Use of Research and Evidence in Education (CUREE) June, 2003.

Cordingley, P., Bell, M., Rundell, B., Evans, D., and Curtis, A. (2003) *The Impact of Collaborative CPD on Classroom Teaching and Learning: How does collaborative continuing professional development (CPD) for teachers of the 5–16 age range affect teaching and learning?* London: University of London, Institute of Education, EPPI-Centre eppi.ioe.ac.uk/EPPIWeb Content/reel%5 Creview groups%5CCPD%5Ccpd rv1/CPD rv1.pdf)

Corrie, C. (2003) *Becoming Emotionally Intelligent.* Stafford: Network Educational Press Ltd.

DfES (2003a) *Transfer and Transitions in the Middle Years of Schooling (7–14): Continuities and discontinuities in learning.* (Brief No: 443 (June)). London: DfES.

DfES (2003b) *Speaking, Listening, Learning: Working with children in Key Stages 1 and 2* (0623-2003 G). London: DfES.

DfES (2003c) 'Booklet 3: School organisational factors and the management and deployment of resources' (0758–2003 R), *Behaviour and Attendance: In-depth audits for primary school.* London: DfES.

DfES (2003d) 'Booklet 4: Continuing to improve the quality of teaching and learning through classroom-level factors' (0758–2003), *Behaviour and Attendance: In-depth audits for primary school.* London: DfES.

DfES (2004a) 'Excellence and Enjoyment: learning and teaching in the primary years' in *Primary National Strategy: Professional development materials*
- Understanding how learning develops; Learning to learn: Progression in key aspects of learning (0524–2004 G) (5)
- Creating a learning culture
  - Conditions for learning (0523–2004 G)
  - Classroom community, collaborative and personalised learning (DfES 0522-2004 G) London: DfES

DfES (2004b) 'Unit 10: Group work' (DfEs 0433–2004 G), *Pedagogy and Practice: Teaching and learning in secondary schools.* London: DfES.

DfES (2004c) 'Unit 17: Developing Effective Learners' (DfES 0440–2004 G), *Pedagogy and Practice: Teaching and learning in secondary schools.* London: DfES.

DfES (2004d) 'Unit 18: Improving the climate for learning' (0441–2004 G), *Pedagogy and Practice: Teaching and learning in secondary schools.* London: DfES.

DfES (2004e) 'Unit 19: Learning styles' (DfES 0442–2004 G), *Pedagogy and Practice: Teaching and learning in secondary schools.* London: DfES.

DfES (2005) *Excellence and Enjoyment: Social and emotional aspects of learning (SEAL)* Cross-curriculum materials (0110-20058 G). London: DfES.

Ekman, P. (1999) 'An argument for basic emotions', in T. Dalgleish and M. Power (eds), *Handbook of Cognition and Emotion*. Chichester: John Wiley & Sons pp. 169–200.

Elias, M.J. and Zins, J.E (1997) *Promoting Social and Emotional Learning – Guidelines for educators*. Alexandria, VA: Association for Supervision and Curriculum Development (ASCD).

Fry, P.S. and Ghosh, R. (1980) 'Attributions of success and failure: comparison of cultural differences between Asian and Caucasian children', *Journal of Cross Cultural Psychology, 11 (3)*: 343–63.

Fullan, M. (1991) *The New Meaning of Educational Change*. London: Cassell.

Futurelink (2005) *Supporting SEAL: Social and Emotional Aspects of Learning*. Bristol: Futurelink Publishing. (Tel: 01275 331300)

Gardner, H. (1983) *Frames of Mind: The theory of multiple intelligences*. London: Fontana Press.

Goleman, D. (1995) *Emotional Intelligence: Why it can matter more than IQ*. New York: Bantam Books.

Goleman, D. (1998) *Working with Emotional Intelligence*. New York: Bantam Books.

Goleman, D. (2000) 'Emotional Intelligence', paper presented at the International Conference on Emotional Intelligence at Hilton Hotel, Chicago, 21–23 October. Chicago, IL: Linkage.

Goleman, D. (2000) *International Conference on Emotional Intelligence presentation paper* Chicago, IL: Linkage

Hargreaves, L. and Galton, M. (2002) *Transfer from the Primary Classroom – 20 years on*. London: RoutledgeFalmer.

Izard, C.E. (1971) *The Face of Emotion*. New York: Appleton-Century-Crofts.

Johnson, D.W. and Johnson, R.T. (1999) *Learning Together and Alone: Cooperative, competitive, and individualistic learning*. Boston, MA: Allyn and Bacon.

Lakin Phillips, E. (1978) *The Social Skills Basis of Psychopathology*. New York: Grune and Stratton.

Ledoux, J. (1992) 'Emotion and the limbic system concept', *Concepts in Neuroscience*: 2.

Linn, M.C. and Burbules, N.C. (1994) 'Construction of knowledge and group learning', in K. Tobin (ed.), *The Practice of Constructivism in Science Education*. Mahwah, NJ: Lawrence Erlbaum Associates.

Maines, B. and Robinson, G. (1999) *You can...you KNOW you can!* Bristol: Lucky Duck Publishing.

Maslow, A.H., et al. (1999) *Toward a Psychology of Being*. John Wiley & Sons: Chichester.

Mayer, J., Salovey, P., and Brackett, M. (1997) *Emotional Intelligence: Key Readings on the Mayer and Salovey Model*. Port Chester, NY: National Professional Resources, Inc.

Miller, J. G. and Bersoff, D. M. (1992) 'Culture and Moral Judgment: How are conflicts between justice and interpersonal responsibilities resolved?', *Journal of Personality and Social Psychology, 62 (4)*: 541–54.

Morris, E. (2001) Insights Primary London: NFER-Nelson

Morris, E. (2004) *Emotional Literacy and Resilience Profile*. Gloucester: School of Emotional Literacy Publishing.

Morris, E. and Scott, C. (2003) *Whole School Emotional Literacy Indicator*. Gloucester: School of Emotional Literacy Publishing.

Morris, E. and Sparrow, T. (2000) *Post Graduate Certificate in Emotional Intelligence Programme*. Gloucester: Centre for Applied Emotional Intelligence.

National Healthy Schools Standard (NHSS) (2004) 'Promoting emotional health and wellbeing through the National Healthy Schools Standard', accesssed online at: www.wiredforhealth.com

Petrides, K. V., Frederickson, N. and Furnham, A. (2004) 'The role of trait emotional intelligence in academic performance and deviant behaviour at school', *Personality and Individual Differences*, 36: 277–93.

Shoda, Y., Mischel, W. and Peake, P.K. (1990) 'Predicting adolescent cognitive and self-regulatory competencies from preschool delay of gratification', *Developmental Psychology*, 26 (6): 978–86.

Walker, M. and Casey, J. (2005) *Developing SEAL: Building on the Primary Strategy*. Bristol: Futurelink Publishers.

Weare, K. (2004) *Developing the Emotionally Literate School.* London: Paul Chapman Publishing.

Webb, N.M. (1991) 'Task-related verbal interaction and mathematics learning in small groups', *Journal for Research in Mathematics Education,* 22: 366–89.

Winston's Wish (2005) *Supporting a Bereaved Child or Young Person: A guide for professionals.* Accessed at www.winstonswish.org.uk

INDEX